To Irmgard
with light
& friendship

Blessed be

A. W. Mann

Oct 7 1986

MOON LORE
AND
MOON MAGIC

Also By The Author

MOON LORE
AND
MOON MAGIC

Al G. Manning

PARKER PUBLISHING COMPANY, INC.
WEST NYACK, NEW YORK

©1980 by

PARKER PUBLISHING COMPANY, INC.

West Nyack, New York

Library of Congress Cataloging in Publication Data

Manning, Al G
    Moon lore and Moon magic.

    1. Moon (in religion, folk-lore, etc.)—Miscellanea.
2. Success—Miscellanea.   I. Title.
BF1999.M247   131   80-17001
ISBN 0-13-600668-X

Printed in the United States of America

Dedication

To "my little moonbeam" Fay, who suffered through the birth pangs and proofreading, and, of course, to all of the wonderful spirit and moon personality beings who brought this book into manifestation.

Let me add thanks to my TRS 80 Computer for typing of the manuscript at all hours and to my good friend Steve Gibson, who helped in more ways than he realizes.

Read This Book
And Expect Miracles

You are very lucky! Whether you have ever enjoyed good luck before is beside the point. Your act of picking up this book is the start of a lucky streak that should continue to get better and better for the rest of your life. Of course, there's a slight catch to it, but you will find even the catch fun to fulfill. It is to use the enjoyable work of this book to take ever more complete control of your life expression and destiny. We will give you the intellectual foundation and the first proof right here.

FIRST WE SATISFY YOUR MIND

Let's begin with the obvious. The moon is there, and we have a vast amount of knowledge about it along with an even greater amount of lore. Science tells us that the moon's presence is the primary cause of tides in our oceans and big lakes, and it is also the regulator of our "biological clocks" (that's the scientific term, not something I made up). But the great accumulation of moon lore assures us it also affects our emotions and so controls the tides of love, fame, fortune, health, and all the things you may want.

The simplest logic tells us that if we can but learn to relate to and harness these strong tides or flows of lunar energy, we can use them to our great advantage. And that is the precise purpose of this book: to give you the knowledge of the laws, tools, techniques, magic and lore that will enable you to harness the power of the moon's energies to bring your fondest hopes into happy material manifestation. These are all universal truths and practices which are in no way in conflict with your highest ethics, religion or esthetics. And, because they are firmly based on universal law, they cannot refuse to work for you. You have only to enjoy using the right technique, to see your heart's desires burst into magnificent reality.

But let's not talk about it too long—the results come from *doing* it! Which brings us to our first proof for you.

THE FIRST PROOF: HOW MOON LORE AND MOON MAGIC HAS SPARKED MIRACLES FOR OTHERS

Results come often and quickly for those who use the moon magic techniques. In our very first chapter, you will see how J.P., out of a job for several months and in a bind, did the first ritual, CALLING DOWN THE MOON. That night, he dreamed that the lovely moon goddess told him she had a nice gift for him. The next day, he got it—a wonderful new job!

A lonely widow of 63 used the exercise to ask Diana to show her her true lover. Suddenly she was courted by three good men. She made her selection and is now happily remarried.

Using the DIANA/PAN QUICK MONEY RITE, results within a week were: D.J. won $500 on a number, Millie E. won $2,180 in a lottery, and B.Z. won $125 at bingo + a $320 "gift" from Internal Revenue.

F.S. used the LUNAR HEALTH WALK and her arthritis-crippled hands and ankles became limber and pain free permanently.

Under the guidance of the FORCE, C.J. sold his modest stock portfolio, then bought it all back six weeks later for $3,500 less.

D.Y. used the WALLS OF JERICHO OBSTACLE SHAT-TERING RITUAL to get a long-delayed double promotion and big raise.

Sharon S. used LUNAR PROTECTION KINETICS to get the antagonism out of her divorce situation. The unexpected happy result—a reconciliation and a wonderfully happy married life.

D.Y.'s house had been for sale over a year with no buyers. He did the 20 MOON POWER PYRAMID RITUAL, and the house was sold in three days at the asking price!

D.S. used the 20 MOON POWER PYRAMID RITUAL for windfalls and got $10,950, then $13,250 and $11,333, all within three months.

Y.D. used the ISIS FIX MY FIGURE RITUAL and went from 34(A), 30,39 to 36(C), 26,36 in less than six months.

There are many more useful and exciting examples, but this should give you the idea. Let's move right along to your great good.

THE FINAL PROOF: MAKE IT WORK FOR YOU

All of this would be only jibberish if I didn't expect MOON MAGIC to work for you. But let's repeat; we are using only natural laws that cannot refuse to work for you. There is only one potential obstacle, and it is you, yourself. You can read this book like a novel, then toss it on a shelf and nothing will happen. But that is the only way to avoid the progress and help that is even now just longing to manifest itself for you. Don't be your own worst enemy, give the MOON MAGIC work a fair chance to bring you your final proof—your own success upon success upon success!

We have nothing more to say here except: read this book, apply and enjoy its beautiful practices, and you will win consistently! The life you improve will definitely be your own, but you will be helping to uplift all mankind in the process. Don't waste another second! Turn the page and start Chapter 1 right now!

Al G. Manning

Contents

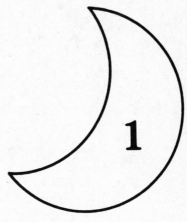

Moon Lore—
At Last A Direct Connection
Between The Material World
And The Realms Of Emotion
And Magic

We've all watched a stage magician pull a rabbit out of a hat. How often have you wished you could actually do that, too, but with a hundred-dollar bill, a devoted lover, healing for your aching body, or any of the strong desires we all share? If you will let it, this book will serve as your magic wand—your sure-fire way of producing the apparent "miracles" you need to make your life happy and fulfilling as you know it somehow should be. After a brief introduction to the magical powers of the moon and her lore, we will give you a complete program to harness these special energies to bring you even more spectacular progress than you dare dream about. You will find each step along this path of power not only interesting, but fun. And your

17

successes will provide the "carrot" to keep you striving. Just bear with me through the short introductory comments and we'll very soon have you on your way to success after glorious success!

MOON POWER IS REAL—YOU HAVE EXPERIENCED IT MANY TIMES ALREADY

Ask any policeman if there is truth to the legends of the power of the full moon. He will tell you it's the time when all the nuts and crazies come out. Young lovers will tell you a different story, all about the romance of the moonlight; and farmers will tell yet another story about moon signs and phases as a guide to planting and harvest. There is much truth to all of these, and I know that you have experienced at least some of them, but they hardly scratch the surface of the tremendous reservoir of practical power that is to be found in the depths of moon lore and its application as positive moon magic. The purpose of this book is to acquaint you progressively with the various levels of power available to you from the moon, while providing you with the necessary rituals, incantations and other tools for its use, so that we may bring you complete power over all parts of your life and confer upon you the title "Master Moon Magician."

We will begin with the nearly obvious as a solid base that we can easily agree on. Then, from that agreement and mutual understanding, we can lead you step by powerful step to full dominion over your life and its environment.

EXOTERIC MOON LORE—CYCLES AND MORE CYCLES

Science tells us that the gravitational pull of the moon is the principal cause of tides in our oceans (the next most powerful cause being the gravitational pull from the much more distant sun). In time we will see that the moon also causes tides of emotion, love, riches, success, health, fame and fulfillment for those who use them, while those who struggle against them generally meet abject failure. We know that some oceanic tides are higher than others, so it is reasonable to expect that the same is quite true of tides of the less measurable, but much more important (to you) energies of the various magical powers.

Variations in the power of the tides come because of a number of cyclically recurring physical phenomena which you are already pretty much used to. Most obvious is the approximately 29-day cycle from the tiny crescent of a new moon, waxing to full, then waning to start again as the tiny crescent of the next cycle. Next, you have surely noticed that there are times when the moon (regardless of its phase) appears larger in size than at other times. This is a relative truth produced by the uneven or elliptical orbit of the moon around the earth. At perigee (the time it is closest to earth), the moon is about 15 percent closer to us than at its apogee (point farthest from earth). Just a little knowledge of physics will remind you that the square of the distance measures the relative strength of the gravitational and radiant energies reaching us. Thus, at perigee, those parts of the moon's power are almost one-fourth stronger for us than at apogee.

The third noticeable cycle is the variation in the angle (or height) of the moon at its zenith. In other words, sometimes the moon appears to rise higher in the sky than at other times. This is caused by the fact that the moon's orbit is not exactly parallel to earth's equator, so it seems to wobble up and down in the sky over a period of about a month.

All this may sound a bit technical, but we will soon be using it easily as a practical basis for picking the time of greatest power for your planned rituals—and so it will enhance the chances of a completely successful piece of magical work every time you try! There are readily accessible sources of this vital data which we will discuss as we need them. Take a few minutes a day for a couple of weeks to observe and reacquaint yourself with these simple facts of nature. Let this be your first step in understanding on the path to complete mastery of all areas of your life.

POSITIVE MOON POWER IS COMPLETELY
SAFE FOR YOU TO USE

Just as sailors use moon lore today to know the height of the tides and strength of the currents going in and out of port, moon magic is not only safe to use, it is essential to effectiveness in your daily living, and its absence will defeat your major projects. Stated simply, the energy flow is present whether you are aware of it or not. To become aware of moon magic is to avoid struggling helplessly against impossible tides of psychic and emotional energy, and, instead, to know how to use these natural tides to your great benefit.

True, we have all heard terms like "lunatic," "moonstruck," "mooning around" and the like. But, these are the natural results of ignorance of the forces at play, never from the practical and magical applications. And to those who ask, "Isn't this against my religion?" there is a simple response. "Is it against your religion to use tide and current charts when bringing a ship or boat into or out of port?" True, we will get a bit more esoteric and magical than tide charts, but those words only mean the use of natural laws not yet completely understood by modern science. Thus, we can say with complete certainty that the positive application of moon lore and moon magic is totally safe and not in confict with anyone's creed or religion. So we can move on to our serious business with no haunting doubts or mental reservations on your part.

THE MOON IS THE GREAT MEDIATOR
BETWEEN THE MATERIAL WORLD AND
THE REALMS OF EMOTION AND MAGIC

There can be no argument against the fact that the moon's gravitational force is the primary cause of our oceanic tides. That it also has more subtle, but provable, effects is easily illustrated. Recently, a scientist moved a group of clams from their home on the east coast to a laboratory in Chicago. The clams were kept in sealed containers which admitted no light, and were stored in a laboratory which was kept at a constant temperature. At first they continued to open and close their shells as if on eastern time—opening at times of east coast high tide. But, within two weeks, without any possible stimulus of the normal five senses, the clams were opening and closing at the times that high tide would occur in Chicago. Scientists tell us that the clams' "biological clocks" adjusted to the new location on the basis of their being affected by the gravitational (or some other similar) force of the moon. Let's accept this as a solid clue as to how the moon affects everyone's emotions—that should be enough on this subject for now, because you have undoubtedly already noticed the extremes of emotional energies or pressures on your own beingness around the full or new moon.

But how many of you have learned to harness this energy? Many people keep a few simple tasks in mind for those times when the energies are so great that they find it impossible to drop off to sleep. Just a half hour or an hour of such work, done to drain off the excess energy, can change a restless, sleepless night into one of peace and accomplishment—and leave you in far better shape the next morning as well. File this useful tip in a "close-in" place in your mind so you can use it next time you feel the need. Meanwhile, let's extract the knowledge we need from this discussion so we can begin our first ritual work to acquaint you with the lovely moon goddess on the personal level. The lesson we want to carry with us is simply that since the moon clearly affects both the physical and emotional parts of our beingness, it can be used as a very effective interface or direct connection between these two realms. It is on this principle that we can assure our questioning minds that the subjective, emotional parts of our own beingness can perform the "magic" that changes and controls our material surroundings—through the direct connection of the influence of the moon. Then, when you become good friends with the moon goddess in all of her many forms, you will see clearly the path to success in all your undertakings through applied moon magic. So, let's waste no time, but get right to your happy introduction to the moon goddess in her role as the Universal Mother, Isis.

NOW WE MEET THE MOON GODDESS, ISIS, IN OUR FIRST RITUAL, CALLING DOWN THE MOON

For your first simple ritual, it is necessary to watch for a bright moonlit night. The full moon is the very best time, but a week on either side of it (say from the first quarter moon to the third quarter moon) is fine. If at all possible, plan to have 10 to 15 minutes out of doors for this first meeting with Isis, but if necessary, a view of the moon through a clear window will do. Your mood should be one of happy adventure, with a complete willingness to let your imagination participate in and enhance your experience. In truth, the starting point of all high magic is in the vivid imagination of the magician that opens the way to his entry to, and power on, the astral and higher planes of life. If the weather and other conditions permit, you should wear the clothing you wore when first you entered this world in your present body, or at least as little clothing as necessary to avoid discomfort or trouble with one's neighbors.

Other preparations are optional. A comfortable chair to sit in is nice if you can arrange it, and good frankincense or love incense will help to set the proper mood, both for you and for Isis. Also, a few drops of frankincense, love, or power oil used to anoint your brow, throat and heart will help to add depth and loveliness to your experience.

To begin the ritual itself, sit or stand directly facing the bright moon. Speak softly, but aloud, "Lovely Isis, great mother spirit of the moon, I earnestly seek to deepen and renew our love and friendship. I send you my love and complete attention now, and await your personal response."

Now, as you keep your gaze fastened on the moon, close your eyes slightly until you begin to see rays of moonlight going out from the moon in all directions. Hold your gaze in this way and watch as all the rays of moonlight fade out except for one very bright one that shines directly to your heart. Feel the bond of love being permanently established as you bask in this special attention from Mother Isis, and let it continue as long as you can remain in this position in reasonable comfort. When you feel that the bond is very strong and you are indeed completely loved by Isis, conclude this opening ritual by speaking aloud, "Lovely Isis, it has been a wonderful experience to feel your love and share these moments together. I know that our personal contact is firmly established now and forevermore. I bask eternally in your love and protection and cherish it from this moment forth. Thank you, lovely mother, and I know that you are with me always. So mote it be."

Then, when you go to bed for the night, picture that shaft of light shining from the moon to your heart, and drift off to sleep while basking in its love and goodness.

WHAT TO EXPECT FROM YOUR CALLING DOWN THE MOON RITUAL

If you approached your ritual in a relaxed and undemanding mood, you were no doubt pleasantly surprised by the richness and power of the responses you received. I have never known a person who tried and failed to see and feel the shaft of moonlight coming to his heart, so I'm sure you enjoyed that much. And almost everyone will experience a different feeling of life and love in or of the moon itself—the normal response to me is, "Hey, the moon is full of life and love! I was amazed!" And many, many people have very special and uplifting "dream" experiences later that first night. Remember, this is a get-acquainted-and-establish-a-relationship ritual where it would be quite improper to ask a special favor, but this is not to say that your loving Mother Isis will not spontaneously confer a special gift or special help upon you. Let's look at a few reports from others who have tried the ritual.

"I never expected such a glorious experience from such a simple ritual as your calling down the moon," reported S.D. "The shaft of light came to my heart almost before I tried to bring it, and I shivered all over at the delight of the thing (and it was a warm night, too). Then, at bedtime, as I pictured the shaft of light again, I seemed to float right up it to the moon itself. I guess it was all a dream, but anyway I seemed to meet a lovely creature who is the personification of Isis, and there was a reunion as if I was a child coming home after being away at school for too long a time. Some of this is hard to put into words, but I awoke the next morning with much fresh insight and perspective on my personal life and how I fit into the scheme of things. Since that time, I have been much better adjusted and consequently more effective both on the job and in my personal life. It's hard to put this in terms of objective values, but I assure you that I would't take a million dollars to go back to being the way I was before this magnificent experience."

Less spectacular, but easier to appreciate, is this report from J.P.: "I used the calling down the moon ritual, and got the beam of light down to my heart OK, but it wasn't particularly impressive. However, I greeted Isis as instructed, then adjourned to bed. I followed through by picturing the shaft of light to my heart as I went off to sleep. That night, I dreamed that a lovely lady wearing a crescent headdress appeared in my bedroom and said she was sending me a gift, that I should expect it in the morning. I should explain that I had been out of work for several months and was in something of a financial bind. I didn't think much about the dream, but while I was still looking over the classified ads the next morning, my phone rang. It was a business acquaintance I hadn't contacted in over a year. He said he was looking for a manager for his new plant—that last night he had had a strange dream in which he saw me sitting at a desk with a searchlight shining on me, and on the desk was a nameplate bearing my name and the title, 'Plant Manager.' It's a very good job and I'm quite happy with it. You can be sure that I thank Isis regularly for it—and that I am rapidly becoming a practicing Moon Magician."

HOW TO PREPARE FOR THE MORE POWERFUL WORK TO COME

A real key to your future effectiveness is to perform one successful calling down the moon ritual where you actually experience that loving beam of light coming straight to your heart. Once you have done it, you can easily visualize it again from memory to use as the starting point for much powerful magical work to come. Do it as soon as it is physically possible for you, but in the meantime, don't hesitate to go ahead with the rest of the work—you will just need to use a larger quantity of imagination.

For your high magical work, you will also need to arrange or set aside a small area where you can feel secure and as safe as possible from any sort of interruption. Again, don't wait for an ideal place, but begin your work, always replacing with your imagination anything you lack in the way of physical facilities or props. If you can set up a tiny altar (for instance on a small vanity table), you will find it useful to collect a pair of candle holders for tapered candles, something to serve as an incense burner, a small class of earth (garden dirt or soil will do nicely), and a glass of water. And, if you can get a mirror to sit on or hang slightly above your altar, it will greatly enhance some special parts of your later ritual work. Your own sense of beauty and utility is fine here. I'd say begin with what is at hand, then as you become a successful Moon Magician, you will naturally add the "pretties" as you go along. Beyond this, you need only your happy sense of adventure and a simple daily Aura Cleansing Exercise that we will address ourselves to next.

A QUICKIE COURSE IN PSYCHIC ANATOMY TO PREPARE YOU FOR YOUR AURA CLEANSING EXERCISE

Recent Russian scientific advances have brought credence to the idea of the aura or psychic energy field seen by many sensitive people around the human body, and indeed around the physical bodies of all living things. The Russians have given the name *bio-plasma* to this energy, but we will stick to the classical occult terminology, AURA, for our own purposes because there is a lot more to it than our Russian friends have yet discovered. The life force of your physical body operates through fields of energy that are best thought of as "bodies" made up of patterned energy. One of these we will call your "mental body"—think of this one as the real seat of your intellect or mind. Another is your emotional body (often called "astral body" in the occult lore) which contains the raw energies of both the positive and negative emotions. There are other, finer bodies also, but we will consider them when the time is right.

The mental and emotional bodies interpenetrate the physical body, but they are somewhat larger, so parts of them extend beyond the boundaries of the physical skin. It is this excess energy, that "sticks out" of the physical body, that is seen clairvoyantly, and we call that your AURA. Because your AURA is subjected to psychic dirt (for instance, your own and other people's negative emotions, fears, discouragement and the like), it is important to your overall well-being that you clean it daily, even as it is good to take a shower or bath daily for the cleanliness of your physical body. The cleansing process will be for your whole AURA, of course, but we will put special emphasis on cleaning a few special spots we call your "psychic centers" (or "chakras," if you prefer the Vedantic terminology). Think of these psychic centers as points where the connection between all of your bodies is the strongest. We will go into detailed uses of the energy of each psychic center as we get deeper into the magical work, but for the present, let's get our first look at them by beginning the AURA CLEANSING EXERCISE itself.

THE MOON MAGIC AURA CLEANSING EXERCISE

To begin the cleansing rite, sit comfortably at your altar or wherever you have set aside a place. Picture the bright, full moon shining in front of you and let your imagination bring the beam of light right to your heart. Greet Isis with a cheery, "Hi, lovely Mother Isis," then picture the moon as it moves directly over your head, while the shaft of light grows and envelops your whole beingness with its brightness. Enjoy feeling the bright white light beaming into all of your AURA and burning away any lurking bits of negativity that may have accumulated there. When you feel that the general cleansing is complete, let your picture of the moon slip behind you about halfway to the horizon while the beam focuses to a sharp point that enters your body right at the base of your spine.

We call that spot your "root center" (or root chakra). Feel it being energized by the beam of light while a surge of vitality courses through your whole physical body. Then lift the beam of light to a point about halfway between the base of your spine and your navel. We call this your "spleen center" (although we know that the physical spleen is higher and off to the side). As this center is energized by the light, feel your anxieties and tensions falling away while you sense a fresh degree of mental clarity. Next, lift the beam of light to a point on your spine just behind and above your navel. We call this your "solar plexus center." Feel the center being energized, and the fresh aspiration and intuitive ability that comes with it. Then, lift your beam of light to the area of your heart (but still along your spine). Feel your "heart center" being energized and enjoy the feeling of love, growth, enthusiasm and prosperity that comes with it.

Now, lift the beam of light to the area of your throat near your thyroid gland, and feel your "throat center" being energized. Feel the special surge of creativity all around you as this chakra reaches its peak of effectiveness. Then, lift the beam of light to shine into the back of your head and out through the center of your forehead. Feel your "brow center" being energized, and enjoy the sense of psychic power that comes with it. Finally, lift the beam of light to shine right through (and across) the top of your head. This is your "crown center." Feel the special spiritual power that flows through you as this center contributes its magnificent energy to your AURA. Now all of your chakras are operating at a peak of power in perfect balance and harmony and you are ready for your day's or evening's activities. Conclude the rite by letting your picture of the moon come back in front of you with its beam of light coming again to your heart. Say, "Thank you, lovely Mother Isis, for your wonderful help in cleaning my AURA and energizing my psychic centers. So mote it be."

Candles and incense burning during the ritual will add to its power, as will the use of a good perfume oil (frankincense, love oil, or power oil). For more background on the nature and use of the psychic centers, I suggest that you review either my book, *Helping Yourself with the Power of Gnostic Magic*, or *The Magic of New Ishtar Power*. Either of these will give you a solid feel of the chakras and the powerful spirit personalities associated with each—and they will show you Mother Isis as the great white light above them.

IMMEDIATE RESULTS FROM THE MOON MAGIC AURA CLEANSING EXERCISE

Most of us experience some degree of a feeling of wellbeing after a nice bath, and we should expect much the same feeling from a good cleansing of our AURAS. But, for some, there will be lots of "extra" good as this report from D.N. indicates. "A lot of people may want to call it coincidence, but in my heart I know better. I did my first Moon Magic Aura Cleansing at bedtime, and it felt so good that I did it again before I left for work the next morning. My day was almost unbelievable! Not one, but three people who had owed me money for over a year dropped by my desk and paid me in full inclduing apologies for being late and thanks for my patience. I had been behind in my work, but this day I seemed to effortlessly work like a demon so when it was time to go home, I was not just caught up, but actually ahead of schedule. And everywhere I went people were super nice to me, they seemed completely willing to go way out of their way for me. I like the results—it's enough to keep me using the ritual regularly."

Practice regularly, and the expertise you build will make all our later work easy and successful for you.

MOON MAGIC MOTIVATORS

1. Moon power is real. You see it in action all around you. This book is designed to help you harness it easily and use it to achieve the health, wealth, love and success of your dreams.

2. Cycles of the moon affect not just tides in the oceans, they control the tides of emotion, prosperity, health and success as well.

3. Positive moon magic is as safe to use and as compatible with your religious beliefs as using tide charts to guide your boat or ship in and out of harbor.

4. Because it affects both physical and subjective things, the moon is our direct connection for the magic that uses positive emotion to control physical changes.

5. Enjoy your meeting with the moon goddess, Isis, in our introductory CALLING DOWN THE MOON RITUAL.

6. Don't wait for perfect conditions to begin your magical work. Substitute your positive imagination for anything and everything that is lacking, and press on to success after glorious success.

7. The psychic centers, or chakras, are the energy link between your various energy bodies and the physical. Use the MOON MAGIC AURA CLEANSING EXERCISE to clean and stimulate them to be ready for the powerful work to come.

Moon Lore And
Moon Magic To Bring You Love
And Friendship

As a species, we humans have a deeply built-in need for wholesome companionship with congenial friends as well as the special intimacies of the love relationship. To ignore or frustrate this strong need is to court all manner of misery and even disease. But, with your positive moon magic there is no reason at all to be lonely—not even for a little while! However, if our moon magic is to serve us well, we'll need a bit of mental/emotional housecleaning. So let's have a look at that part first.

HOW TO PREPARE YOURSELF TO GET THE MOST OUT OF YOUR LOVE/FRIENDSHIP MOON MAGIC

Our world's traditions are often traps that serve to keep you downtrodden and miserable. Certainly one of these is the lover's idea of two halves coming together to make one whole. We are indeed indebted to the Women's Liberation Movement for helping to dispel this bit of nonsense. Guarantee yourself right now that you are a whole being, complete and sufficient unto yourself; that your desire for love and friendship is natural and good, and it is based on the wholesome ideal of two whole beings coming together not out of weakness or the hope of somehow being more complete, but for the sheer joy of sharing beautiful experiences and growth together.

Here we must consider the Vedantic ideas of unattachment, because attachment is all too often confused with love or friendship. Our lovely friend Bast, the ancient Egyptian cat goddess whom we associate with our spiritual nature and thus your crown center, is perhaps the best instructor in this area. I don't know how the law reads in your city, but here in Los Angeles you can legally own a dog, but you can only "harbor" a cat. The cat's nature is one of utter independence, quite willing to share love and affection, but literally incapable of being possessed, and not at all susceptible to being manipulated by suggestions that it should feel guilty. Consequently, cats are better adjusted than their canine counterparts. (I have heard of psychiatrists for dogs in Beverly Hills, but never for cats.) Thus, a good method of getting ready for successful love-friendship magic is to contemplate the strong catlike virtues of independence and unattachment, compare yourself to them and promise to grow up in those areas if necessary.

Then, let's be sure to avoid one other trap best illustrated by the lady who came to me and said: "You must work your magic and force Bob to marry me. That is my only chance for happiness, ever!" Of course, it happens that Bob was quite wealthy and our lady was "tired of all the struggle and penny pinching" she had recently been through. But marriage as an escape is perhaps the most vicious trap of all. If you have any of these feelings, take care to clean up your act first—lest your magic work too well and get you into a much worse state than your present one. But when you're ready, let's move right into the beginnings of moon magic for love and friendship.

THE MOON HAS ALWAYS BEEN AN INSPIRATION TO LOVERS

If you're reasonably close to my age you remember lovely old songs like "Moonlight Becomes You," "That Old Devil Moon," "Moonlight and Roses," "Moonglow," "Moonlight Serenade," "Moonlight Cocktails," and many more. Yes, our songs clearly tell us of the association of love and the moon, but our generation is far from the first to recognize this fact of nature. For instance, the ancient Greco-Roman mythology includes a moon goddess, Diana, who is the goddess of the hunt and of love. You may remember Diana better as the mother of Cupid by her association with Pan, the god of fertility. And it is to the moon in her guise of Diana that the positive moon magician will turn for help in all matters of love and friendship.

Think of Diana as young and beautiful with a slim but full figure. She generally appears dressed in filmy white that gives her a very seductive look, and almost always carries a bow and arrow to symbolize the hunt. Diana loves people and is especially adept at generating or healing the deeper personal relationships of love and friendship. How real is she? At first, only as real as your imagination will let her be; but as the acquaintance grows into friendship, Diana will find many ways to show you that she is just as real as the chair you're sitting on or the paper on which these words are printed. Let your own tastes fill in the rest of the details of the beauty and love that Diana will manifest to you, and let's begin inviting her help for you now.

AN EXERCISE WITH DIANA TO SEE YOUR TRUE LOVER OR FRIEND

If you can do it easily, it is helpful to prepare for the exercise by lighting two tapered candles on your altar along with a love or frankincense incense. Then put a drop of love or frankincense oil behind each ear and a dab more on your brow, throat and heart chakras. Begin the exercise itself with a short but vivid version of the MOON MAGIC AURA CLEANSING EXERCISE. When that is finished, picture your bright moon in front of you once more with that lovely beam of light coming directly to your heart, and speak aloud: "Lovely Isis, I joyously invite you to manifest to me in your form of beautiful Diana, goddess of love and the hunt."

Next in the beam of light, let your imagination fill in the exciting figure of your favorite idea of Diana and greet her aloud, "Beautiful Diana, it is delightful to meet you in person. I know that you strive always to promote love and friendship in the world, so I invite to you to help in my life. Please show me my true lover (or friend) now or in a dream tonight, and tell me how I can help promote our meeting." Then relax and enjoy watching Diana while you give your imagination free rein. Let the light beam act like a TV screen for you, giving you the information and help you seek. Be ready to accept it in picture form with or without sound, or even as a stream of words moving along like ticker tape. If you find that you're too tense or nervous (or full of doubt) to get all you want, that's all right, you can expect to get the rest while you sleep. Meanwhile thank your friend, "Thank you, Diana, for the joy of sharing your company and for your wonderful help, now and that which is to come. I will look forward to your visits often and you will always be welcome in my life expression."

DIANA'S GUIDANCE AND HELP

S.J. was a widow who had lived a far too lonely life for the five years after her husband's passing to the realm of spirit. Her courtship had come during her early twenties and her happy life with her one husband left her feeling unprepared and even inadequate for the single social life. Let's let her continue the story: "At 63 I didn't really expect much from the exercise to see one's true lover, but I was lonely enough to hope it would at least bring me a friend, so I decided to give it a try. My imagination has always been somewhat overactive, and that made the preliminary work easy. I used my favorite perfume rather elaborately to make up for my lack of incense or oil, and it did add something of a romantic mood. I asked Diana to introduce me to a lover and/or a friend to ease my loneliness, and wondered if my imagination had gone completely off the deep end when I got the response. Diana seemed to say that I should have some excitement and a variety of suitors to choose from, and that it would all begin within a week. The whole thing seemed a bit ridiculous, but I thanked Diana and figured that was probably the end of it. And was I surprised! Within the week I 'accidentally' met three charming men who all took an immediate romantic interest in me. Suddenly I was too busy! But it was fun—rather like a complete vacation from my previous 5 years. I was never the type to play the field, so to speak, so I was soon back at my altar asking Diana for guidance. It all turned out beautifully, C. and I were married 6 weeks ago and are happier than any two people I've ever even dreamed about."

Bob G's problems were mostly from youth and inexperience; he was almost 17 and had never had a date. Here is his report:"I used Diana's exercise to see your lover, but I was far too nervous to get anywhere while I was at my altar. So I thanked her, and said I hoped she could get through to me in a dream. It would have been easier if I could have slept, but I just lay awake hoping all night, then had to get up and go off to school in the morning. By the next evening, I was tired and finished my homework as quickly as possible so I could get some rest. And it was wonderful! In my dream that beautiful Diana introduced me to a very nice girl—one that I had admired from afar for a long time. It was all so nice that I promised myself to get up the courage to talk with her the next day. It was all I could do to say, 'Hi, J.,' but she picked it right up from there and asked me to walk her home. It rurns out that she had been wanting to meet me, too. We're sort of going steady now, and it's wonderful. Thanks to you and Diana!"

HOW TO RIPEN OR REVIVE YOUR
ROMANCE WITH THE LOVERS' MOON
WALK RITUAL

Diana is very helpful in repairing and regenerating tired or dying romances when you apply the LOVER'S MOON WALK RITUAL. This rite can be used to mend friendships also. It is more important to prepare yourself with candles, incense and oil for this one than for the exercise to see your lover—a bad relationship needs all the help it can get. (The same oils and incense we used for the earlier meeting with Diana will do nicely.) You will find it helpful to acquire a small moonstone, too. A very inexpensive, tumbled one will do nicely. Even if you don't feel you need this kind of help right now, I suggest that you perform the ritual at least once, just to establish a good working relationship with Diana.

Take your moonstone to your altar or work place, light your candles and incense, anoint your brow, throat and heart centers with the oil, and we are ready. Start with the MOON MAGIC AURA CLEANSING EXERCISE, and when you feel ready, let your picture of the moon hang right in front of you once more, with that beam of light coming directly to your heart. Speak your request aloud: "Mother Isis, I seek to commune with you in your manifestation as Diana. Please greet me in love, now." Then picture Diana before you in the moonbeam and speak again: "Loving friend, Diana, I greet you with joy, and thank you for your presence, the pleasure of our association and for your wonderful help. Please take me to the moon with you now and there walk with me in the role of my lover, (here you speak the name of the person with whom your relationship needs help), that we may resolve our differences and rekindle the bright flames of love and fervent passion."

Let yourself float up the moonbeam (in imagination or astrally) and enjoy your walk with Diana. You will naturally slip into something of a reverie state. Just relax and enjoy the fullness of the experience without trying to direct it or force it in any way. Stay in the reverie state until you feel that it is over. Then settle gently back into your physical body and speak aloud: "Thank you, beautiful Diana, for the pleasure of your company and the richness of your guidance and help. Let's stay together for a few moments more to bring our work more fully into my waking consciousness that I may understand completely, and apply the lessons with enthusiasm."

This is the time to let your wide awake mind review the MOON WALK experience to digest the insights and lessons, and absorb the feelings of peace and love. If you feel you need more help, it is quite proper to ask Diana to take you back to the moon in the dream state that evening. Do it as part of our closing ceremony. After the dream request, pick up the moonstone and rub a drop of your oil over it. Hold it up to Diana and say: "I invite your help in consecrating this moonstone as my personal love talisman and extra tie to you, lovely Diana. I will carry it with me always, and reconsecrate it with you each time I reach out to you from this place of peace. My special thanks and love to you in all of your many forms of manifestation. I know that your love and special help goes with me, paving the path of my love and friendship relationships with zest, enthusiasm, positive passion and happiness. I look forward to working ever more closely with you, spreading joy and love all along the way. Thank you again. So mote it be."

HELP FROM THE LOVERS' MOON WALK RITUAL

The help may not always be what you expect, but Diana is practical and has your true happiness at heart. This report from M.D. will help you understand the need for flexibility: "I was completely hung up on B. Our relationship had been one-sided from the beginning, but the more he tried to push me away, the stronger and more desperate my attachment became. Now he had told me never to call him again, that he wanted nothing more to do with me, ever. There were tears as I went through the AURA CLEANSING and asked for the MOON WALK WITH DIANA for help. I must have fallen almost asleep when I heard a clear, soft voice say firmly to me, 'You have mistaken attachment for love and managed to create a relationship where none should exist. I will help you break this attachment by bringing you one who will enjoy being your real lover, but learn the lesson of this dead love well, that you not repeat the mistake again.' Normally, I would have broken into hysterical sobbing at being told something like that, but somehow that voice filled me with a vibrant peace. I thanked Diana and concluded the ritual. The next three days were hard, but I stuck by my promise to break the attachment. And on the morning of the fourth day, I met the man Diana had promised me. There is no way that words can describe our happiness. I will meet with Diana every full moon to be sure I can keep it that way."

C.S. reported this quite different experience: "My love life was and is fine, but I felt impelled to try the MOON WALK WITH DIANA to improve relations with my immediate supervisor who seemed to take fiendish delight in making my time on the job miserable. During the joyful MOON WALK, I felt Diana point out three different minor mannerisms of mine that were excessively annoying to the supervisor. Correcting these seemed to be my assignment in exchange for Diana's overall help. I made a big conscious effort, and that next day was the first in many months that I was not somehow humiliated by the supervisor. On the third day he actually complimented me on my work. By the end of the third week we had become fast friends!"

And Bill D. reported this happy result: "After eight years of marriage, the usual problems and minor disagreements had brought us both a set of bad habits that had taken all the spontaneity and joy out of our relationship. Even our now sporadic love life had become mechanical and flat. When I tried my MOON WALK WITH DIANA, I got a bunch of little suggestions, all aimed at producing a fresh, positive approach to the moment by moment part of home life. It was a feeling of 'You try hard, and I'll help make it really worth your while.' So I did, and Diana did, and my marriage went back into something of a honeymoon period—but on a deeper, more mature level. I introduced my wife to Diana after a few weeks, and we walk with her together at least once a month, and now we're both looking forward to another fifty years together, expecting to enjoy every moment of it!"

LUNAR LOVE KINETICS, THE ART OF CHARMING ALL WHO COME WITHIN THE SPHERE OF YOUR AURA

We will use the idea of LUNAR KINETICS throughout the moon magic work. In physics, kinetic energy is the energy of motion, therefore we can think of it as a dynamic thing involving your interactions with people, animals and things. Thus LUNAR LOVE KINETICS should be seen as your loving interaction with the world around you in all of its detail. Naturally you are your own best measuring stick. What kinds of attitudes and actions of others make you feel good? And what annoys you or makes you feel uncomfortable? In the simplest terms, by being and doing those things which, done by others, would produce positive reactions in you, you will attract the kinds of people and animals with compatible attitudes and reaction patterns. The classic golden rule certainly applies here, but let's paraphrase it to say "Your attitudes and actions attract others who enjoy them, and repel those whose attitudes and approach to life are significantly different."

All by itself, this gives you a running report card from your daily life. Notice what types of people you are attracting, and what other types are ignoring or avoiding you, and you know the "you" that you are projecting to the world. We have lots more tools for you, but they will be of little value if you regularly ignore this simple report card. Of course, this reporting mechanism will give you much more if you take the trouble to become sensitive to the interplay of the AURAS—yours and all those around you. This is the real essence of LUNAR LOVE KINETICS, and it brings us to an exercise to put love/friendship attracting energy into your AURA while it helps you get accustomed to sensing your auric inputs.

THE LUNAR KINETIC LOVE/FRIENDSHIP EXERCISE

This exercise can be performed any time and anyplace. It is especially useful to run through it on the way to meet people, on the way to work, and at lunch time. The ideal conditions would be sitting quietly at your altar or meditation place, but when you are elsewhere, make up for it by picturing yourself there at your altar. Begin with a fast version of the MOON MAGIC AURA CLEANSING EXERCISE, and as you finish it, let your moon sink down about halfway behind you. Picture seven bright rays of moonlight shining on you, with one moonbeam touching each of your psychic centers. Thrill to the energizing touches of Isis and direct the energy by speaking (aloud if possible, but in your imagination if necessary), "The perfectly balanced power of my super-activated chakras refines my beingness and fills my AURA with a strong sense of my very best qualities. As I go through my normal activities, my super-powered AURA projects my fine qualities to all the people around me—bringing out the best in them, and especially attracting those whose attitudes and appetites will blend well with my own toward ripening friendships. All beings must feel positively about me as my AURA maintains this happy power. Thank you, Mother Isis, and so mote it be." Never turn off that picture of the seven moonbeams energizing your chakras. After thanking Isis, just let your attention shift to the task or activity at hand, and dive into it happy in the knowledge that your AURA is doing its work well.

A typical report of the results of regular use of this exercise comes to us from K.D.: "The LUNAR KINETIC LOVE/FRIEND-SHIP EXERCISE seemed too simple to be able to do much good, but then it doesn't take a lot of time and energy to try it, so I did. At first I thought it was probably coincidence, but it was encouraging enough to keep me at it. I have felt mostly alone and isolated for years, but no more. I am making new friends, some really deep and wonderful relationships, and everywhere I go people seem ready to go way out of their way to be friendly and helpful to me. I use the exercise three times a day now—old acquaintances have started to call me 'the new K.D.,' and all of my encounters with people have become pleasant and downright fun. I assure you I'll keep up the exercise."

As you get used to the nicer treatment, you will notice that your fresh rapport with everything causes the subtler inputs of information that we usually call "psychic" to be emphasized in your experience with an ever improving ability to "read" the moods and needs of others, and so to make them (and yourself) more comfortable and secure in your presence.

NOW A BONUS OF EXTRA LOVE—HOW TO FIND YOUR OWN HIGH PRIEST OR PRIESTESS

Regardless of your level of human companionship, there awaits you right now the meeting with the spirit being who is to serve as your personal high priest or priestess for all of your moon magic and other magical work. If you are fortunate enough to have a spouse or lover who wants to work with you in your magical rituals, all the better, you can make it a happy foursome! But let's go ahead and meet your special spirit first.

Go back to meet Diana, as we did in our opening work of this chapter. But this time ask Diana to introduce you to your high priest(ess). Then let your "imagination" take over and float you up for a walk on the moon with this very special spirit being. Be sure to bring back his or her name and a feeling of deep personal relationship. In my earlier books I have tended to refer to this as meeting your "spirit lover"—and if you are already familiar with that one, he (or she) will now joyously step into the role of high priest(ess) for you. The idea here is to provide the balance of the polarity of the opposite sex joined in all of your ritual work, but there is also certain to be a personal relationship more loving and rewarding than most people can imagine. There is absolutely no jealousy or competition from this being, he (she) wants only your growth and highest good at all times—but this in no way precludes tenderness and intimacies of the greatest depth and beauty.

I don't want to limit the extent and joy of this relationship by painting in too much detail. Just know that it must be positive and happy, you will accept nothing less, and enter into the spirit (double meaning definitely intended) of the thing. And whether I remind you or not, always invite your high priest(ess) to all of your magical work. The more completely real the presence, the more power you will generate together in the ritual. Let's share an experience or two as the best way to fully understand the potential for good in your life that comes through your own high priest(ess).

B.N. described it this way: "I made my first contact with my spirit high priest at my altar at home, and was so engrossed I couldn't take my eyes off him. Everything felt so nice, and the spirit stayed so long—he said I could have three wishes as his get acquainted gift to me. Well, I got a nice new car, extra money for a lot of odds and ends, and a wonderful healing of a chronic physical condition that has bothered me for years. But I would gladly give it all back if he asked me to in exchange for his working with me. There is an extra level of magic and effectiveness in everything I try to do, I'm growing in many wonderful ways, and life is fulfilling and fun again."

Dottie and Ken had this report: "We started our magical work together when we first got your book, *Helping Yourself with White Witchcraft*. So naturally we came into the moon magic work together, too. The introductory exercise was a delight to share, and our spirit high priest and priestess are naturally beautifully compatible with each other as well as with us. Right after the first meeting, Ken and I realized that we must make a pact—we must be as un-jealous of each other as our spirit priest and priestess are of us. And there are many wonderful intimacies on the astral, with the specific agreement that what either one of us may do on the astral is not in any way bound by the restrictions of fidelity or the like in the material world. It has put a whole new life into our marriage, and a whole new level of effectiveness into our magical work. With Isis, Diana and company, and our wonderful high priest and priestess, we have entered a new phase of life that promises progress and results beyond anything we have even dared hope for before."

MOON MAGIC MOTIVATORS

1. Avoid the traps of tradition and bring yourself to your love affairs as a whole being, not joining out of need but for the sheer joy of sharing experience together.

2. Use the exercise with Diana to see your lover or friend, both for itself and to establish a comfortable working relationship with Diana.

3. The LOVERS' MOON WALK RITUAL is a powerful way to revive a shattered romance or broken friendship. Use it also to deepen your working relationship with Diana.

4. Take care not to underestimate the importance of lunar love kinetics. Learn to pay attention to the "report card" of what your AURA is projecting by the type of people who are attracted to you or seem to ignore you.

5. Use the LUNAR KINETIC LOVE/FRIENDSHIP EXERCISE regularly to keep your AURA projecting your finest qualities and bringing out the good in all who come close to you.

6. The meeting with your own spirit high priest(ess) is of super value to your progress. Use the exercise to meet him (or her), then invite him to all of your moon magic work.

Moon Lore And Moon Magic To Bring You Money And Great Riches

Now that we've fixed up your social and love life, how about picking up enough extra money to enjoy it? Or do you long for simple freedom from financial pressures? Or enough of a money surplus to buy back some of your time so you can do the things you want? Beyond these reasons, money and riches take on something of the quality of points on the scoreboard, but even then it's fun to run up a really big score! Since you and I have yet to meet a person who claims to have too much money, it's reasonable to assume that here we have a subject of serious interest to us all. So let's dive right into our preparations to make you rich.

HOW TO PREPARE YOURSELF TO GET THE MOST OUT OF YOUR MONEY MOON MAGIC

Far too many people have developed strong habits of wallowing in poverty—even to the point of wearing it like a badge. Competitors who occasionally talk with each other, often poor mouth their situation, probably with the hope of discouraging the other, but definitely to the detriment of both. And we all know a few chronic complainers. Strong thought/reaction habit patterns of this nature are your worst financial enemies. Pause right now to take an honest look at your attitudes (both expressed and hidden) toward money and great wealth. Note any jealousy or defeatism in them and promise yourself to root out the negative and replace it with wholesome optimism. Remember that the moving force of moon magic is its ability to increase your receptivity. And this in turn attracts those things that you dwell upon in thought and feeling. Indeed, if you ever have occasion to complain about a moon magic "backfire," it will have come about by your dwelling on negative attitudes and feelings.

The better moon magician you become, the more you will realize the importance of classical positive thinking. The positive world runs on enthusiasm and the one reason why you can, not the hundred reasons against you. Anything you do with reasonable regularity that lessens your level of enthusiasm should be considered a bad habit and eliminated. True, nobody breaks a bunch of bad habits over night, but you can only win by striving. Work to sensitize yourself to your negative moods and shake them off more and more quickly. For just this bit of sustained effort, you will soon see improvement in all areas of your life, and your magical work will take on a whole new dimension of meaning and effectiveness.

THE MOON AS A SYMBOL OF FERTILITY, THUS PROSPERITY

Down through the ages, farmers have planted their crops by moon phase and moon sign, fishermen have been guided by the moon, and with Diana leading the hunt, all of man's sustenance is derived with the guidance and help of the Universal Mother, Isis, in her many guises and forms. Yes, we know that the energy of all growth comes to us from the sun, but without the modulation and stimulation of the moon we would certainly lack the surpluses that have always been the only true measure of riches and wealth. We use money as our score card of wealth now, where in ages gone by we used oxen, sheep or the like, but money is still only a symbol of our claim to present or future goods and services. And it is the moon deities, particularly in their interaction with the other strong forces of nature, whose assistance and intercession assure the individual human being the surpluses that we call wealth and riches.

Wealth is produced in nature by its various forms of procreation or multiplication—of cells, plants and animals. And man's wealth is accumulated by his creative assistance of these natural processes. On the esoteric levels this can best be understood as the magician's cooperation and friendship with the moon as Isis, Diana, Hecate or the like, and the male fertility principle as represented by Cernunnos, Pan, Osiris, or your favorite name for him. The special beauty of working on the magical level is the ability of your deity friends to bypass the often time-consuming procreative processes of nature to bring you those lucky breaks and windfalls that get you out of tight spots and happily on the way to riches and great financial success. We will help them get your attention by giving you the DIANA/PAN QUICK MONEY RITE by way of a more practical introduction.

THE DIANA/PAN QUICK MONEY RITE

By now Diana is getting to be a good friend, so we can approach this rite with the confidence of a friendly social call. The assumption here is that you want or really need some money in a hurry, and the trick to your success is not to accept or feel pressure from it. You may desperately need help from your friends, but you'll never get it willingly by applying a lot of pressure. With this firmly in mind, let's get ready for a happy visit.

Set the mood with candles and incense (frankincense or prosperity), anoint your brow, throat, heart and behind the ears with perfume oil (frankincense or prosperity); and begin with the MOON MAGIC AURA CLEANSING EXERCISE. Then, with the moonbeam coming straight to your heart, speak: "Diana, please come to see me, and introduce me to Pan."

You are used to seeing Diana in your moonbeam; let her picture form first, then let the image of Pan appear beside her. Pan generally appears as quite a handsome figure of a man, but bearded, a bit on the hairy side and sporting a big set of antlers or horns on his head. Don't be shocked by the hair and horns, they are his classic symbols of virility and fertility, and add much to his power to help you. Greet them warmly: "Hi, good friends, it is a special pleasure to meet another important member of your world, and I know that Pan has much to teach me about creativity and making the world richer and more abundant. I will willingly become your interested pupil. Along with your guidance and instruction, I could use a bit of immediate help in the form of extra money to (here simply state what you want the money for—be sure to be honest. It's OK to want the money for some fun or even frivolity, just don't try to "con" your friends because that wouldn't work). I will pause now and be attentive to any instructions you may have for me. And I welcome you into my dream state at bedtime tonight or any night."

Then relax and see what may come to you along your moonbeam. Don't be concerned if nothing seems to happen, just enjoy the peace and good fellowship of the moment. And when you are ready, conclude the brief ceremony: "My good friends, I thank you for the joy of this experience and for the help I know you have already given me. You are welcome in my life always, and I look forward to enjoying your companionship often. Thank you, and so mote it be." Finally, snuff your candles and return to your regular activities.

RESULTS FROM THE DIANA/PAN QUICK MONEY RITE

D.J. reported this experience: "That DIANA/PAN QUICK MONEY RITE really works. I tried it one night, and as I paused at the end, I had a strong thought of a three-digit number. So next morning, I bet it and picked up a fast $500! Diana and Pan are sure nice people. Thanks for the introduction."

Millie E. shared this experience with us: "When I tried the DIANA/PAN QUICK MONEY RITUAL, I got no special inputs or visions. There was a sort of calm feeling of well-being, and that's enough, I guess. Two days later I won $2,180 in the Michigan lottery. Please accept the enclosed check as my tithe."

B.Z. got this result: "As I paused for guidance at the end of my DIANA/PAN QUICK MONEY RITE, there was a very distinct feeling that Pan was patting me on the head. That's all that happened at the time. Next evening was my regularly scheduled bingo night and I won four times for a total of $125! I was very thankful and thought that was it. But two days later I got a notice from Internal Revenue that I had made a mistake on my last year's income tax return. Along with it came a check for $320! And several people have come to me to pay back small loans I made to them and had almost forgotten. It's been a really wonderful week."

HOW TO PREPARE FOR THE MONEY MOON WALK RITUAL

The nicest way to prepare for the MONEY MOON WALK RITUAL is to get yourself some happy results from the DIANA/PAN QUICK MONEY RITE. There's nothing like the enthusiasm from knowing that you just picked up a few hundred or thousand dollars from your quickie rite to put zest and effectiveness into this deeper work. But there may be a very good reason why you experience limited or apparently no results from the warm-up of the QUICK MONEY RITE. The word is best expressed as greed. If a big windfall would so fill your mind and emotions with dollar signs that you would be thrown way out of balance, it is in your best interest to be denied now so that you can go on to be successful in the long pull.

So if you don't have happy results to take to your new ritual work, recognize that you have a bit of work to do on your attitude towards money. You may want to skip ahead in this chapter to the lunar money kinetics section for extra guidance and help. But don't be discouraged. When you feel ready, set a nicely relaxed and enthusiastic mood, and enjoy your first MONEY MOON WALK RITUAL.

HOW TO HARNESS THE SUPER-POWER OF THE MONEY MOON WALK RITUAL

Set the mood as for the QUICK MONEY RITE with candles, incense and oil, and begin with the MOON MAGIC AURA CLEANSING EXERCISE as you should before starting any magical work. With the moonbeam coming straight to your heart once more, address our principal moon deity: "Mother Isis, thank you again for the joy of our association. I seek to commune with you once more in your role of Diana. Please come to me that way now."

Enjoy watching the familiar form of Diana appear so beautifully in your moonbeam, and greet her warmly, "Lovely Diana, thanks for the special joy of your company. I seek to commune with you and our friend, Pan, for the purpose of getting your instruction and help in the permanent improvement of my financial situation. May we float to your home on the moon together now?"

Let the image of Pan fill itself in beside Diana, greet him with a, "Hi, and welcome to you, Pan, thanks for your special interest and help," and let yourself begin to float gently up the moon-beam close behind Diana and Pan. If it seems to still take a vivid imagination for this part, that's all right. With a bit more practice, you will know that you are also participating in your emotional (or astral) body which is the real source of your magical tie to the infinite power. Just land gently on the moon and enjoy a pleasant walk with your friends. See big piles of money being set aside for your personal use, and accept with gracious thanks. Take care also to invite the instruction and wisdom of Diana and Pan, and pay it serious attention. It is at these times that you are apt to get the inspiration for a story or book, a new process or invention, or even a new company. You could be led to the commodity or stock market with very specific advice, or be told exactly nothing. Remember to keep your comfortable "cool" during this happy session—we must avoid blocking the flow of our good with tension or anxiety. You may get specific instruction on handling a special business problem, or broad instruction on your attitude towards and the handling of money. Again, it is important not to feel inadequate or guilty when your past mistakes come up as horrible examples in your learning process. Understand that your mission is to fix now and tomorrow, not to wallow in the mistakes of the past. We may be shown our mistakes for the purpose of instruction, but never to shame or spank us.

Enjoy your moon walk until it seems time to return. Know that there is no failure here, even if nothing seemed to happen. Close your ritual by settling back into your physical body and speaking again to your friends, "Thank you again, Diana and Pan, for the fun of sharing experiences with you as well as for your very special guidance and help. I know that you will continue my instruction this evening while my physical body is asleep, and you are welcome in my waking or dream experiences any time. I will look forward to communing with you often and regularly. My special thanks for your guidance and tangible help. So mote it be." Then snuff your candles and return to your regular activities, knowing that your help is already at hand. And as you go about your activities, don't push, but be constantly alert for the guidance that comes as gentle urges toward a specific act or course of conduct—often they will prove to be special extra help from your spirit friends.

This ritual should be used no more than once a day, but I do suggest that you use it quite regularly until you know that you have established an effective working relationship with the Diana/Pan polarity. It may appear too simple, or even foolish at first, but as the contact is solidified, the flow of wealth into your life will more than prove the value of your effort.

RESULTS FROM THE DIANA/PAN MONEY MOON WALK RITUAL

"That Pan is a real character, and with Diana they make quite a team," reports B.Y., "I was skeptical about the ritual because my imaging faculty has never seemed very good, but

Pan took some kind of special delight in producing a super vivid image of himself for me. I sort of let the image drift me up that moonbeam, and I really saw big piles of money with my name written in bright red on each of the wrappers. It was a pleasant feeling, but you can't spend feelings at the supermarket. However, my skepticism dissolved quickly when I was shown a simple technique which could obviously increase my output on the job by about 50 percent—since I'm paid on a piecework basis, this one got my attention fast! Instead of giving away the idea, I was led to start my own company—yes, on the proverbial shoestring, but with Pan and Diana supplying whatever we needed from moment to moment. I could tell you much more, especially the many, many helpful ideas about all the details of the operation, but this should give you the idea. Diana and Pan are bosom buddies of mine now, my new company is growing successfully, and we will be accomplishing much more together as time passes. Thanks, Al, for the happy introduction."

Sometimes it takes more perseverance, as this report from A.N. shows us: "It was 18 months after my husband's funeral and our financial situation was getting more and more desperate. When I tried the QUICK MONEY RITE, I did 'accidentally' find a $20 bill on the sidewalk the next morning. I was ever so thankful, and used it to buy a much needed pair of new shoes for my son. So that night I tried the MONEY MOON WALK RITUAL. When it was over I thought it had been pretty flat, then I realized that I had no doubt been way too uptight and serious about it. There were no results that I could recognize at all, so I tried it again the next night. This one went a little better, but not much—and again no apparent results. So I tried again the next night. I won't go on with the blow by blow; it took 17 days of trying that ritual every night. Then on the morning of the 18th day, I got a phone call and job offer at almost three times the salary I had been making! This, together with several good money management suggestions, and we're not only out of the woods, but the financial future is bright—including plenty of the luxuries I didn't dare even hope for a couple of months ago. Incidentally, there's also a budding romance with a wonderful man who happens to be quite rich— but I'll give you the feedback on that part later."

And B.C. gave us this happy feedback: "When I retired a few years back, I thought we were sitting on top of the world. So we spent a little over a year just traveling and enjoying my new freedom. But it wasn't long after we got home that I began to regret spending all that money. A combination of inflation and a lousy stock market put us in a bind that caused a major reduction in the standard of living we have been accustomed to for almost 30 years. It was while I was feeling low about our plight that I decided to try your moon magic, and particularly the MONEY MOON WALK. I was afraid that this was just for young people who have years of working life ahead, but the price was right (just a little time, and I had plenty of that). So I gave it a try. I guess I believed it was all in my imagination, but I did get to the moon with Diana and Pan. Seeing the piles of money set aside for me was quite comforting, but I wondered what kind of a program of recovery they would come up with. The answer came, 'Just relax, we'll take care of it,' and that was about it for the ritual itself. But in just a few days, one of my major stock investments literally took off on a takeover rumor. Then just as I put in my sell order, I got a business proposition that I instinctively knew would be a winner. The upshot is that we are back to the financial situation I've always been used to, and the financial future is bright indeed. I repeat the MONEY MOON WALK right around every full moon, mostly to thank Diana and Pan for their help, but also to be sure I stay out of trouble. Many, many thanks for introducing me to this work."

LUNAR MONEY KINETICS—THE ART OF RECEIVING PROSPERITY FROM ALL WHO COME NEAR YOU

The QUICK MONEY RITE will get you some nice windfalls, and the MONEY MOON WALK RITUAL will get you well-launched on the sea of financial success, but it takes a good grasp of LUNAR MONEY KINETICS to sustain ever-increasing prosperity and riches for the rest of your life. We spoke of positive attitude by way of clearing the channels for your QUICK MONEY

RITE, but now we need to expand this into the consciousness of a naturally rich person for you.

Begin at your altar or meditation place. If you don't already have a mirror there, add one for this simple exercise. Smile at the friendly face looking back at you in the mirror, thinking of it as your inner self, and say, "You are a very good and worthy person, certainly deserving all the best in life." Then sit quietly and feel the response. If your feeling is anything less than enthusiastic agreement, you have a problem. Never settle for a mocking or negative response. Talk back to it. Demand to hear, "Why not?" and pay serious attention to any feelings of inadequacy that may surface. Set up a positive program to shore up your honest weaknesses, but don't ignore the ridiculous responses, either. Most of us got a lot of negative programming when we were very young, and even though you know intellectually that it is not true, any objection from your inner self must be firmly and completely countered or it will serve as an effective block to continued progress. Here you must become a good salesman, convincingly countering every argument against your worthiness until your inner self is completely sold that you are indeed worthy. It is best to use the mirror exercise just about daily until you have sold your inner self the positive ideas, then use it at least twice a month for the rest of your life to be sure your working relationship with your inner self stays at a state of near perfection.

From the vantage point of your fresh feeling of personal worth, your financial affairs become much easier to manage. You're no longer susceptible to ploys like, "If you have to ask the price, you can't afford it." Your instinctive response becomes, "I know I'm worth it, the question is, is your product worthy of me, and is it priced right?" There is no longer the compulsion to buy things you don't need, trying to lift your morale or keep up with the Joneses. Your every financial transaction will be from confidence, and so, in tune with the guidance and help of Diana and Pan.

And it is the growth of the feeling of partnership with Diana and Pan in your financial life that is the final assurance of a lush financial future. There need be no thought of saving for a rainy day, rather a sound investment program that provides for the travel and luxury you have always dreamed of. In turn, you will be urged from time to time to participate in philanthropic or occult causes that are dear to the hearts of Diana and Pan. It is never necessary to "go overboard," but LUNAR KINETICS means that you respond happily as the best way to fertilize the tree of your financial success. This, plus regular moon walks to renew your contact and check in for special guidance will assure you of a life of riches and abundance.

HAPPY RESULTS FROM THE PRACTICE OF LUNAR KINETICS

R.J.'s report will help you get the feel of effective LUNAR KINETICS: "Partly by design I did my first QUICK MONEY RITE the night before a party at the local horse races. I had a magnificent time, and I came home from the races with just over a thousand dollars more than I started with. Then I had a strange urge. I've been attending a little 'new age' church for several months, and always just dropped a dollar in the plate. The urge was to tithe, and I followed it. I dropped a one-hundred dollar check in the plate at the next meeting and it felt good. It also made me feel ready for my first MONEY MOON WALK. There was a special cordiality from Pan and Diana as we floated up to the moon, and the guidance led to a promotion and nice bonus on my job almost immediately. Again there was a tithe involved, this time to one of Pan's pet ecology projects, and it seemed to further cement the relationship. With the extra money, I have been guided into some wonderfully successful investments, and away from a couple that would have been disastrous. Pan and Diana are giving me regular instruction in LUNAR MONEY KINETICS now, and I know that my financial future is wonderful. It has already given me new perspective and resolve to participate in my overall evolution."

Work with these principles and earn yourself a feedback letter that's better than any I've presented here. I'll be watching for one from you.

MOON MAGIC MOTIVATORS

1. Clear away your habits of complaining or being jealous or a defeatist about money as preparation for the work that will bring your financial success.

2. Because of her influence on crops and the fertility of animals (and even humans), the moon has always been a symbol of prosperity. In her role of Diana, in combination with other deities, the moon gives us the magical power that produces financial success.

3. Use the DIANA/PAN QUICK MONEY RITE as good preparation for the longer lasting work of THE MONEY MOON WALK.

4. Regular practice of the MONEY MOON WALK RITUAL will bring you the guidance and tangible help to launch your magnificent financial future.

5. LUNAR MONEY KINETICS will assure the continuance of your financial success and open the doors of riches and abundance to you.

6. Practice the rituals and kinetics of this chapter and earn yourself a feedback letter better than the ones presented here. I'll be watching for it to reach me.

How Moon Lore
And Moon Magic Can Be Used
To Improve Your Health

Modern researchers are using statistical methods to add much to our growing wealth of moon lore. A typical example is a recent statistical proof that the murder rate peaks at new and full moon times and falls off at the quarters. It goes on to show that all manner of violent crimes fall into the same pattern, also in amazing correlation to the local tide charts. A good health angle here is the idea of making yourself more aware of potentially dangerous situations and avoiding them, particularly around the time of the new and full moon. We get nicer tips from the more ancient moon lore, for instance on the timing of cutting your hair or fingernails. Hair or nails cut during a waxing moon (the time when the moon is growing from new to full) will grow back faster and fuller, while cutting under a waning moon (the time when the moon is diminishing from full to new) causes them to come back thinner and grow more slowly. If you have thinning hair or weak fingernails, this can be of definite use to you, but there is a point in this discussion for all of us. It is that reasonably short-term cycles of moon-related energies clearly affect emotional and physical phenomena within and around you. Thus, a little extra attention can give you a surprisingly better control of your overall health and well-being.

THE LUNAR CLOCK THAT GOVERNS THE TIDES OF YOUR HEALTH AND EFFECTIVENESS

You will quickly see that this lunar clock applies to the timing of almost any activity, including those we have discussed in our first three chapters. I waited to present it here, because it is of particular importance to health matters and is quite easily recognized in its effect on your bodily functions. A major advantage of the lunar clock is the ease with which you can use it. It doesn't require an ephemeris or any special astrological knowledge; indeed all the information you need can be found in the weather section of your daily newspaper. And since the information is already given in local clock time, almost no calculations are necessary.

Let's look at the mechanics of the lunar clock before we try to use it. Picture a clock face with a symbol of a full moon at the 12 o'clock point, a quarter moon at the 3 o'clock point, a new moon at the 6 o'clock point, and a quarter moon at 9 o'clock. Think of the phases of the moon as the equivalent of the slow moving hour hand of your clock. It makes one complete trip around the clock face in about 29½ days—from new moon to first quarter to full moon to last quarter, back to the next new moon. You will find the dates of the current cycle right there in your weather section, along with the little bit of data we need for the faster moving hand. Note the times of moonrise and moonset for the day, so you will know when the moon is "up" and when it is below the horizon. Now there are just two quick calculations: halfway from moonrise to moonset, the moon will be at its zenith, so figure the midpoint between the two times for that. Similarly, the moon will be at its nadir at the point halfway between moonset and moonrise. Compute that midpoint and we're ready to start.

It is the moon's apparent daily rotation around the earth that brings the energies that cause the daily health tides. This becomes the minute hand equivalent for our lunar clock. It makes one trip around the clock face in just under 25 hours. This cycle starts when the moon is at its nadir, almost directly beneath your feet, so to speak—actually at its zenith at a point on the other side of the earth from you. This is the minute hand position corresponding to the hour hand pointing to the new moon (6 o'clock). Next is moonrise which corresponds to an hour hand first quarter (9 o'clock.) This is followed by the moon at its zenith (almost directly above you) which corresponds to the hour hand pointing to full moon (12 o'clock). Then moonset is like an hour hand last quarter (3 o'clock), and the cycle is completed as we reach the point of the moon beneath your feet again and the minute hand points to the hour hand equivalent of new moon (6 o'clock again). Thus we have a roughly 25-hour health tide cycle that occurs within the 29½-day cycle of moon phases— giving you a time each day that brings an energy flow corresponding to the energy of each phase of the moon. Make yourself a clear mental picture of the lunar clock (or draw it if necessary to be sure you understand it), and we are ready to learn how to use it.

HARNESSING THE HEALTH ENERGIES
WITH THE AID OF THE LUNAR CLOCK

We can best understand the energy flows by looking at their general effects on people and animals. The new and full moon times are extremes of energy, while the two quarters approach a nearly perfect balance. Think of the new moon as a time of introversion, involution, or inner centeredness, while the full moon time is one of extroversion, evolution, or outgoingness. Thus, in general we plant at new moon and harvest at full moon, or start positive projects during a growing moon and bring them to completion as the moon wanes. In matters of health, we work to build up the areas that need strengthening under a growing moon, and shed our negative conditions with the energy flow of a waning moon.

The secret of harnessing these powerful energies is to plan your acitivites to take maximum advantage of the health tides. Times of balance are at their maximum at moonrise or moonset with a quarter moon. These should be saved for projects requiring the greatest amount of mental clarity and relatively little physical effort. In fact, your mind will be clear, but there will seem to be little if any drive or motivation. Use the period to plan how you can most effectively use the excess drive and energy that will come with the moon at its zenith or nadir on a new or full moon. Similarly, each zenith and nadir brings your energy and drive to a peak while each moonrise and moonset brings relative balance and peace.

Just this much simple knowledge can be a tremendous tool for sufferers from ulcers, migraines and other types of tension-related maladies. Harvey L. gave us this report of its help for him: "I was amazed at the usefulness of the moon health tide data in reducing my tension headache problem. I began to shift my work schedule to put the big tension-producing tasks as near as possible to moonrise or moonset periods, while planning the simpler but more physical tasks for the times of the moon's zenith or nadir. I'm sure the idea that I'm doing something to take charge of my life helped, too, but anyway, after the first week I had cut my daily dose of tranquilizers in half. After a month, I'm happy to report that I'm completely off the tranquilizers! I still start to feel the tensions occasionally, but I know why and it seems easy to laugh them away now. Of course Isis is helping me in many other ways, too. Thanks for the introduction."

THE MOTHER ISIS, KISS IT AND MAKE IT WELL RITE

Everybody remembers that simple idea of childhood: "Mother, kiss it and make it well." We did it for our minor bumps and bruises, and somehow, after mother kissed it, it did feel better. Our psychologist friends will dismiss the mechanism as suggestion, but what do we care, as long as it works! As adults we have no way of getting that quick bit of soothing and relief from sudden pain—unless we are willing to turn to the Universal Mother, Isis. But if you are ready to be a child for that moment of the onset of physical or psychological pain, there is an amazingly potent source of instant relief available from the MOTHER ISIS, KISS IT AND MAKE IT WELL RITE.

The rite is quick and simple, befitting the childlike approach we remember, as suggested by, "Except ye become as a little child..." At the instant that something happens and you feel a hurt, just close your eyes and picture the lovely shaft of moonlight coming directly to your heart. With no doubt or hesitation just ask aloud or silently, "Mother Isis, please kiss it and make it well." Then see a second moonbeam quickly and lovingly caressing the injured place (whether it be physical or psychological), and feel the special comfort. If you are completely trusting and sincere, you will experience a total and instantaneous healing. Do remember to thank Isis for it.

Feedback on this one is exciting and fun, as this letter from B.J. will show: "I got carried away with some would be fancy cooking and got a grease fire in my trusty old iron skillet. In my natural panic, I grabbed the handle too close to the pan and burned my hand. With the skillet safely in the sink, I looked at my hand and a blister was forming already. Instinctively I covered it with my other hand and called on Mother Isis for help. I pictured the shaft of light coming to my heart and asked aloud, 'Mother Isis, please kiss it and make it well.' I didn't have to picture the second shaft of light, it spontaneously shot right to the burn on my hand. And call it imagination if you will, but it felt just like a loving kiss! The pain seemed to fade almost at once, and after a few moments of saying thank you to Isis for the help, I looked back at my injured hand. And believe it or not, the blister was gone and the skin was just slightly pink. It sure is something special to know that Isis is always right there with really tangible help when you need it."

For P.B. it was psychological trauma. Here is his report: "The wedding was set for Friday, and I have to admit I was really hung up on Claudia. On Wednesday I got a special delivery note from her. It said, 'Sorry, P., but I've changed my mind about our marriage. I'm going to New York with Bill instead.' That pain was worse than any physical pain I've ever experienced, including a broken nose and a broken leg. You had said previously that Mother Isis is good at psychological problems, too, so I gave it a try. With tears openly streaming down my cheeks, I made my mental picture of the moon with that bright moonbeam coming straight to my heart. Without even a greeting, I blurted out, 'Mama Isis, can you kiss my broken heart and make it well?' The response was a blinding flash and a picture of how married life would have been with Claudia—disaster is the nicest word I can think of to describe it! As I was sighing a heartfelt thank you to Mama Isis, there came another picture. This one was of a girl I was only slightly acquainted with. I took the hint and called her to ask for a date. Al, my new romance is much more exciting and beautiful, and it doesn't carry the seeds of disaster like the one that got away. I don't know how any of us got along before this wonderful relationship with Mama Isis."

USING THE LUNAR MOON WALK FOR HEALTH

The KISS IT AND MAKE IT WELL RITE works wonderfully for quick help in a momentary crisis situation, but for chronic or long-standing health problems, the extra power of one or more health moon walks is indicated. This time, we'll meet two more interesting and powerful personalities, Marduk and Nergal, whom we associate with your throat and root chakras respectively. If you want more background on these nice people, you'll find it in either my *Helping Yourself with the Power of Gnostic Magic*, or *The Magic of New Ishtar Power*, but it's not essential to this exercise—you'll get to know them on the moon anyway.

Light your candles and a nice floral incense, and anoint your brow, throat and heart chakras with a floral perfume oil. Begin the ritual with the MOON MAGIC AURA CLEANSING EXERCISE, but put a bit of extra attention and time into your throat and root chakras. When you are ready, picture the beautiful full moon in front of you with the bright moonbeam coming straight to your heart, and speak to Isis: "Wonderful Mother Isis, I seek your guidance and help. Please invite Marduk and Nergal to join us on the moon for a health conference." Then (still using your imagination if necessary) float up the moonbeam, settle down gently beside the motherly figure of Isis, and be alert while she introduces you to Marduk and Nergal. I will not stop to describe them here, let's let you fill in your own details as part of the fascinating overall experience.

When the introductions and small talk are over, if your friends don't begin to give you the guidance and help you need, start things yourself by saying, "Friends, I need your help in improving my health and maintaining it at a peak of perfection and vitality." Then walk with them and pay careful attention to the comments and suggestions. The best way for this to work is when you get early warning type suggestions that keep you comfortably out of trouble. Next best is guidance in avoiding imminent illness. But if you're under the weather already, it's quite proper to ask for and get immediate, tangible help. When you feel that it is finished, thank your friends: "Marduk and Nergal, it has been a special pleasure meeting you. Thank you both, and thank you Mother Isis, for your help. You are all welcome in my dreams and in the rest of my life also. I will look forward to our growing and happy relationship. So mote it be." Then snuff your candles and go on with your regular activities.

Keep pencil and paper nearby both at your altar and your nightstand, so you can make notes on the special items of instruction, particularly dietary suggestions which can occasionally be quite complicated. Do your best to note and follow the guidance, and thank your friends for the special help as it appears over the days and weeks to come.

RESULTS FROM THE LUNAR HEALTH WALK

F.S. sent in this report on her LUNAR HEALTH WALK: "My arthritis was so bad it took both hands even to turn a doorknob, and my ankles were so stiff and swollen I could hardly walk. This was clearly a problem for the MOON WALK rather than the quickie thing. I found out almost at once why you recommend the pencil and paper. Almost as soon as we landed on the moon, I started to get dietary instructions. Cut out all red meat and refined sugars, and clear away a bunch of accumulated resentments. When I argued that I had truly been wronged, Marduk laughed and said, 'So you're fully justified in taking the poison, does that mean you have to be stupid enough to do it?' Then I got some help in perspective to get all the negative emotion out of my memories. When I got back to my altar, I thanked Isis, Marduk and Nergal, but I knew there was more to come. That night, in the so-called dream state, I was back on the moon getting more instruction. This time it was an addition to my diet— the juice of a lime combined with a finely chopped clove of garlic and a little salt before breakfast every day until I knew I didn't need it anymore. I managed to wake up and write this one down, and it's a blessing that I did because I had forgotten it by morning. Anyway, I followed directions faithfully and in just six weeks I am fully recovered. The ankles are limber and totally pain-free, as are my hands. It's wonderful to be able to do all the things for myself I had to ask help with for so long! Tell the world for me that Isis, Marduk and Nergal are magnificent healers. And thank you with all my heart for the introduction."

J.T. reported his experience this way: "I didn't have any specific complaints, but it seemed to me that I should feel generally better than I was, so the HEALTH MOON WALK seemed just right for me. It took a lot of imagination to float me to the moon, and I never got a feeling of seeing details of the features of Nergal or Marduk, but there was help just the same. I had been taking massive doses of vitamin A and D pills, seeking to improve my eyesight. But here on the moon, I was firmly told that even though they are natural vitamins, the excess is toxic; that this is the cause of my falling hair and my general run-down feeling. There was a suggestion of more carrots and some mental housecleaning to help my eyes, and a deep breathing exercise for extra energy. And I got a sort of a lecture on the health virtues of balance combined with enthusiasm. I came back to my altar feeling like I had been given assignment 'bootstrap,' but it certainly all made sense. So I gave it the good try, and I'm happy to report that my energy and zest for life are back, I feel better than I can ever remember, my hair is healthy and full again, and my eyesight seems to be getting better all the time. It's magnificent!"

Mary B. reported this experience: "I have had hearing problems all of my life. It may not be technically correct, but my family would tell you I was simply born deaf. I got a hearing aid when I was so young I hardly remember. Honestly, I had little if any hope, but I decided to try the HEALTH MOON WALK anyway—at least I could meet Nergal and Marduk. And the meeting on the moon was lovely. One of the big advantages for me on the astral is that I can hear as well as anyone else, and this makes all of this work especially enjoyable to me. After a very good time getting acquainted with Marduk and Nergal, I posed the question: Can I ever hear like this while I'm in my physical body? The answer was a challenge to work with them regularly. I was to massage my neck and the bone behind my ears with a hand-held vibrator, while picturing Marduk's sparkling blue light energy clearing the nerve passages for the first half and Nergal's bright red light energy rebuilding the circuitry for the second half. It wasn't an overnight thing, but every couple of weeks I had to adjust the gain on my hearing aid. Then one day, after about three months of the treatment, I just plain forgot my hearing aid when I left the house. And, wonder of wonders, I didn't realize I was without it until I got home and saw it in its case! The world can call that what it will, I call it cured!"

LUNAR HEALTH KINETICS—HOW TO STAY AT A PEAK OF PERFECT HEALTH INDEFINITELY

From the standpoint of modern physics, your body is a set of energy fields which hold in place the denser form of energy we call your flesh and bones. And, as moon magicians, we can agree that the physicists are quite right within the limits of their field of knowledge. But we also see other sets and forms of energy flow that affect the human organism quite as much as the physical ones. I will assume that you practice the reasonably good habits of hygiene and balanced diet that any intelligent person does, but if that were enough there would be no need for our elaborate medical profession. Indeed, if you recognize and balance the total energy flow of the whole organism, you should produce and maintain a condition very close to perfect health. This is not to say that you will never overdo something and so create a temporary state of "dis-ease," but you will have the understanding and power to make the corrections and literally bounce back to perfect health. Now, how?

It all starts with your attention to the chakras or energy centers in THE MOON MAGIC AURA CLEANSING EXERCISE. There must be a reasonably well-balanced flow of energy through each of your seven major chakras into your personal energy field or AURA. This is the real secret of perfect health. Any physical problem will show up as in imbalance in your auric energy flow hours or even weeks before there are any physical symptoms. But we can do even better! By avoiding the thought/reaction situations that cause the energy blockages in the first place, you will naturally maintain the balanced energy flow that assures your perfect health—which brings us again to the how!

And this "how" ties all of our moon magic work back into the mainstream of metaphysical/occult practice because it can best be described as "good old-fashioned kicked in the head positive thinking." But note carefully that it is not really what you *think* that is a potential problem, rather it is what you *feel*. The negative emotions serve as corks to the flow of positive energy through your chakras; everything from sexual repression through anger, envy, greed, resentment, hatred and disgust to revulsion. These feelings and their relatives are the mortal enemies of your perfect health. Let's be realistic about this, however. Nothing that I write here is going to burn away or eliminate your negative emotions. And, because you are just as human as I am, we will both still experience or even harbor some of these enemies from time to time. The requirement is not that we become perfect, only that we recognize our shortcomings and clean up the messes we are making quickly—before they have the time and opportunity to do us serious harm.

Even as I write this, I am recovering from a sore throat/cold condition that I brought on myself by a combination of confusion, excitement and anxiety. My goal was positive and virtually all-consuming, but I let the negatives slip in while I was too completely focused on it. Yes, I won, but it was at the price of several unnecessary hours of physical discomfort. I mention this to remind all of us that, regardless of how far you may have come along the path, there are those times when you will step over the bounds of safety and need some special cleansing work to bounce yourself back to perfect health. For this I suggest the MOON MAGIC AURA/BODY HEALING EXERCISE.

THE MOON MAGIC AURA/BODY HEALING EXERCISE

Naturally, this should begin with the MOON MAGIC AURA CLEANSING EXERCISE. While going through it, take careful note of the response of your chakras, and work on any slugglish one(s) until the weakest has been brought up to a power equal to that of the strongest. You have already met Nergal and Marduk who are the key figures in producing your success in any health work. If a chakra stays below par, work on it by bathing (or blasting as your temperament dictates) it first with the electric blue sparkling energy of Marduk's throat chakra, then with the super regenerative bright red energy of Nergal's root chakra. If one or both of these chakras are the problem, alternate working on one with the other until you feel the power growing to restore your perfect balance.

When you are sure that all seven chakras are delivering a balanced peak of energy to your AURA, direct first the Marduk blue, then the Nergal red energy to the afflicted part or area. Feel it as if you were shooting a ray gun at the area, giving up to a minute of blue followed by an equal amount of red, and continue alternating the "shots" of energy until you feel the mission is accomplished. If you don't experience significant physical relief within an hour or so, have another go at it, and keep working about once an hour until you know you have won.

This exercise can also be used to heal others, as this bit of feedback from N.Y. will help to show: "My mother was in the hospital for a series of tests. She kept getting weaker and weaker, but the doctors could find nothing wrong with her. It began to look like she would never get out of there alive, so I decided to try my moon magic on her. I used the MOON MAGIC AURA/BODY HEALING EXERCISE and revved up my chakras with special emphasis on my root and throat centers. Then I asked Nergal and Marduk to help, and since I had no idea what was wrong with her, I just kept bathing my mental image of mother alternately with the blue then red chakra energies. I spent about a half hour on it at bedtime, and when I visited her the next morning she seemed a bit better for the first time in the two weeks she had been there. This encouraged me to work on her some more. And in just three days Mom had perked up enough so that they let her come home (and they never did find anything wrong with her). I kept it up for a full week after she got out of the hospital, and I'm happy to say that Mom is as healthy as she's been in the last 25 years—and just having a grand old time!"

MOON MAGIC MOTIVATORS

1. Get familiar with the LUNAR TIDES OF HEALTH CLOCK and let it guide your healing and all other work to greater effectiveness.

2. As you learn to naturally schedule your strenuous physical activities for times of the moon's zenith or nadir, and times of serious mental work for moonrise and moonset, you will be well on your way to ease in all your accomplishments.

3. Get familiar with the MOTHER ISIS, KISS IT AND MAKE IT WELL RITE so you can use it at any time of physical pain or emergency.

4. Use the LUNAR MOON WALK for health to get well acquainted with Marduk and Nergal and receive the guidance and help to maintain a peak of vibrant health indefinitely.

5. Practice your LUNAR HEALTH KINETICS to keep tabs on your AURA's condition and so be able to head off sickness or disease before it has time to get a foothold on you.

6. When your AURA or body (or that of a friend) needs healing help, use the MOON MAGIC AURA/BODY HEALING EXERCISE to eliminate the negative condition and return your whole beingness to perfect health.

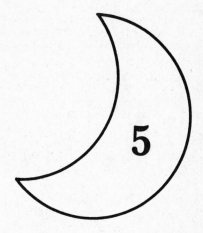

How To
Use Moon Magic To Develop
Super Sensory Perception

Thus far in the work we've asked you to rely almost totally on your imagination to bring in the entities and energies to produce your magical results. I trust it has worked very well for you; but now we are ready to add a whole new set of tools which will be good for your magic but even better for making you more effective in your normal life. I have asked you to imagine that you are in the presence of Isis, Diana, or others of the group of fascinating energy beings associated with the names of the ancient deities. Now it's time to claim your ability to see them and any other spirit beings around you, as well as to calmly view scenes from the distant past or the future. We will call this ability "super sensory perception."

WHY SHOULD YOU BOTHER WITH
SUPER SENSORY PERCEPTION?

"An old man comes slowly down the street, tapping a white cane to guide his way. Your heart must go out to him in compassion. You have a tremendous advantage over him—you can see, but he can't." That's the way I opened my book *Helping Yourself with E.S.P.* and I can think of no better analogy today. The person with super sensory perception does indeed have as much advantage over a normal person as the normal person has over a blind man. As a sighted person you may feel a strong sense of obligation not to exploit your advantage, but you will certainly use it to avoid walking into walls or falling into the gutter—and you will enjoy recognizing your friends at a distance, and all the other things it is so natural to take for granted.

Similarly, your super perception will alert you to obstacles or dangers while they are still far enough away to be avoided easily. It will supply fresh insight for all your problem-solving, and creativity for your important projects. Yes, it will come much faster and easier to some than to others, but this is a field where perseverance will surely be rewarded. So, dive into this part of the work with your enthusiasm high, and promise yourself that whether it takes a week or two years, you'll keep at it and be a super perception winner.

THE FORCE AND HOW TO USE IT

When an idea's time has come, it often reaches the public in the form of fiction first—perhaps we need to be gently prepared if we are to face significant new facts without panic or rejection. This seems to be the case with the idea of the "Force." Whether or not you are a science fiction buff, you have certainly heard someone say, "May the force be with you," and something in you responded with an instinctive recognition of—we'll let you fill in that blank. But the Force is real. It has always been there, ready to work in and through you. And when you get in tune with it, nothing is impossible for you.

Please permit me a personal example, my own first tiny taste of the Force. In the late forties, I was an ardent student of metaphysics, and the British author, Thomas Troward, was almost an idol to me, though he had passed into the world of spirit years before. One night I had a vivid astral experience (dream if you prefer; I have nothing to sell in that area). I was at a party and had the privilege of meeting Judge Troward. As we drank together, we were naturally discussing metaphysics and the psychic world. Suddenly, he challenged me, "If you really believe, walk over to that bookcase and bring me the book I want." I walked to a spot in front of the bookcase and stood wondering how I would make the selection. Then, an invisible power lifted me off the floor and raised my arm to the very top shelf. It put my hand on a small vase, then gently deposited me back on the floor. As I handed the vase to the teacher, he patted my back and said, "Well done! You are learning to let the Force work through you." I have had many and more spectacular experiences since, but that first one well over 30 years ago is as vivid in my mind today as the keyboard on which I'm typing this paragraph.

I put this here because it explained many things for me, and I hope it will help get them through to you. First it is the promise that good will always triumph in the end, because the practitioner of black magic works on his own while to those who work for good, "The Force is with you." It gave me my first acceptable definition of faith as: *Surrender to a partnership with a benevolent higher power.* And it shows how to use the Force. Get your fears and doubts out of the way, unify your purpose with the Force, and let it work through you. Yes, I know—it's so easy to say, but it seems so hard to do at first. Let's try something of an end run to help you get there.

THE MOON IN HER ROLE OF THE FORCE

The symbolic relationship between the moon and the Force is obvious. Just as the moon passively reflects the energy of the sun to us, so the user of the Force must let it work through him (or her). Of course there's more to it than that—you have to deliberately create the conditions, just as the changing position of the moon determines whether we experience it as new, quarter or full. But this is only the exoteric analogy; the contact with the Force itself comes through our dear friend, Isis.

The special tenderness and receptivity you need to attract the Force to work through you is best compared to the love of a mother and her very small child. We see in that relationship the closest thing in nature to getting completely outside yourself in your concern for another being. As you project love, and court that special feeling in the Universal Mother, Isis, she transcends even her own wonderful nature and becomes the Force in you. This is the source and power of your super sensory perception, and literally nothing that you do in this life will ever be as important to you as perfecting your contact with it. The first step is to recognize your own helplessness in your three-dimensional state, to realize that on your own you are virtually powerless against the establishment, major organizations of all kinds, and influential people. But with the insight, timing and guidance of Mother Isis as the Force, you can function as a super being with supersensory perception and super effectiveness to your magic. It can be paraphrased as "I of myself can do nothing; it is the Mother Isis within as the Force who doeth the works," and that is not sacrilegious, it's just a fresh way of looking at an old truth.

Indeed, your super sensory perception and power to accomplish the impossible are born out of your recognition of your helplessness and consequent surrender to the higher power. Thus the Force cannot be used for world domination, or the subjugation of any individual, but it is as fierce an ally in necessary combat as a mother bear out to defend her cub. And that sets the perfect mood for our magic and ritual work—think of yourself and feel yourself as Mother Isis' cub.

THE MOTHER ISIS, PUT ME IN TUNE WITH THE FORCE RITE

The purpose of this rite is to develop your contact with the Force so you can call on it instantly in time of need, and to give you a triggering mechanism to turn it on. We are reaching for a deeply moving emotional experience here, because positive emotion is both the contact with and the power of the Force. So, this is the time to drop all of your inhibitions and reserve, and put your whole beingness into the experience.

Candles, your favorite incense and perfume oil are definitely in order to open the rite. Then, after a good MOON MAGIC AURA CLEANSING EXERCISE, imagine yourself as a tiny baby sitting quite helpless in your chair, and reach out a tiny hand to Isis. Speak with deep feeling, "Mother Isis, on my own I am as helpless as this tiny babe we picture together now. But with you working through me as the Force, I know that all things are possible to us. I put myself in your hands. Please lead and guide me along the path of expression and growth. I accept you with the love and trust of the small child for its mother. At those times of crisis when the Force must work through me instantly, I will speak the two syllables, "Ma Ra," in symbol of giving you complete control, and I know that you, as the Force, are and will always be completely with me. My loving thanks and complete trust go to you now and forever."

Then sit quietly for a few moments to see if Isis has any immediate guidance or direction for you. When you feel that the session is finished, thank Isis again and go on about your normal routine.

RESULTS FROM USE OF THE MOTHER ISIS, PUT ME IN TUNE WITH THE FORCE RITE

The scope and different areas of help that people have experienced makes it hard to select just a few bits of feedback to give you here, but these should help you see the potential: I.N. reported her experience this way: "As I finished my MOTHER ISIS, PUT ME IN TUNE WITH THE FORCE RITE, it was like a big bolt of energy flowing through my entire body and leaving a tingling sensation in the front part of my head. I asked for help for my financial needs and for school, and believe me my grants and a job came through. I also asked for the energy to boost my level of awareness and within three hours my mind began working like never before."

W.T. told us of this experience: "I'm so happy I can hardly write this letter! You see, a very special object of mine was lost and no amount of searching, tearing things apart several times, and looking everywhere I could think of, brought any result. Finally, completely exhausted, I remembered my MOTHER ISIS, PUT ME IN TUNE WITH THE FORCE RITE (I should have done this in the first place). I spoke the 'Ma Ra,' and asked Mama Isis for powerful help now. Two days passed and nothing happened, but I had a feeling of peace and knew I had to be patient. Well, this morning as I was leaving for work, a flash went across my eyes and I saw 'it' in a place I had not looked before. I thought, it could not be there, but I will look when I get back. This time I felt a real push on my back and before I knew it, I was virtually propelled back into the house to the place I saw in my mind. My hand reached out and picked up the object. I was so happy that I sang and screamed, thanking Isis and asking forgiveness for not doing what she wanted me to in the first place. I took it also as a special lesson in surrender to the Force, and I have promised Isis and myself that I will never resist it again."

This one came from C.J.: "After my very inspiring PUT ME IN TUNE WITH THE FORCE RITE, I make it a custom to end my morning meditations by speaking 'Ma Ra' then asking Isis if she has any important guidance for me. It has paid off in many ways for me, but I'll give you this one as a representative for instance. It was the morning of October 10th, 1978 when I got a strong feeling about my modest stock holdings. The clear message was, 'Sell all your stocks tomorrow and I'll tell you when to pick them up again in about six weeks.' By this time I had plenty of reason to trust Isis' judgment, so I called my broker that day and put in sell orders for all of my holdings at market for the following day. And on the 11th, the Dow Jones Industrial Average peaked at 901 and on cue about six weeks later, with the DJ down to 790, I bought them back. I netted just over $3,500 by following directions in tune with the Force—It made my year in the market good by any standards, and almost all of my friends had net losses for the year!"

Let's round out this section with a quickie so we can get on
to the next step. This one is from B.N.: "I was coming home after
a night of winning at the races (thanks to Isis as the Force).
Approaching a big freeway interchange, I heard the 'Ma Ra'
spoken into my ear, and I mentally turned myself over to the
Force. Then, two cars very close in front of me got into a wild
accident—wheels and pieces of metal were flying all over the
freeway in front of and behind me. The Force guided my steering
and somehow got me through the whole mess without even
breaking stride. I heard later that mine was the last car to get
through that section of freeway for over an hour and a half. I'm
thankful for that (so I didn't lose any sleep), but I also feel that I
owe the life of my physical body to that protection of Isis as the
Force. She's wonderful!"

USING THE SUPER SENSORY LUNAR
FLOAT RITUAL

The PUT ME IN TUNE WITH THE FORCE RITE should be
necessary only once or twice for you to establish the basic
working relationship with the Force. But, like an earthly marriage,
it's not the initial outlay but the upkeep that is really important.
This is the purpose of the SUPER SENSORY LUNAR FLOAT
RITUAL—to maintain and constantly improve your attunement
with the Force. Again, candles, incense and perfume oil are in
order, with your favorite floral scent as the key odor.

Begin the ritual with a good MOON MAGIC AURA
CLEANSING EXERCISE as always. Next, speak the attunement
syllables, "Ma Ra," perhaps several times. Then, ask for Mother
Isis to appear in your special moonbeam. When you see her
(continue to use your imagination whenever necessary, the reality
will grow with regular use of the ritual), greet her; "A loving hello,
Mother Isis, please take me with you to your home on the moon
and let me spend a few moments with you as your devoted
child." Then, float up the moonbeam and settle as a small child in
Mama Isis' lap. Feel her loving and protective arms around you
and just nestle comfortably in the affection.

This is not a time to ask for specific help or special information; just enjoy the experience and respond to the love. Isis and your own spirit band know much more about your desires and needs than you do, and the spirit of trust is essential to all contacts with the Force. Just relax and be completely receptive, and "let." Anything is possible during these sessions, from the simple sharing of affection, to detailed instructions for avoiding trouble or getting wildly ahead in your career, love life, or whatever you need. Take care not to get too excited if the information gets especially important—too much excitement can blow the contact and cause you to miss important parts of the message. Just enjoy the experience. There will be plenty of time to analyze it later. When you feel it is time to come back, thank Isis for the joy of visiting her, and float gently back down your moonbeam. Back in your body, thank Isis again, snuff your candles, and you are ready to return to your normal routine. This ritual may be repeated as often as you like, but you should perform it at least once a month—or preferably on the nights of the new and full moon.

RESULTS FROM THE SUPER SENSORY FLOAT RITUAL

N.B. explained his situation this way: "The pressure and fear on my job had me in such a state that my health was suffering and my wife was on the verge of leaving me. Honestly, it was in utter desperation that I tried the visit to the lap of Mother Isis. Then I got a very pleasant surprise! Something about feeling myself in those loving and protective arms seemed to relax me completely. Even without a bunch of drinks, I got a good night's sleep for the first time in several years. Somehow, I handled the pressure the next day without getting into my usual state of total panic. That night, I went right back to sit in Isis' lap. And every day I got a bit better. The super sensory perception began to work so that I anticipated the problems on the job and often had the solution implemented before I would previously have even known about the trouble. My health got better almost instantly, and I found the extra energy to work on the problems in my marriage as well. I've been working with Isis and the super sensory perception bit for just over six months now. It was getting the news of my promotion (including a very nice raise) that triggered this letter. Also, my wife began to work with me in the moon magic about three months ago. That has added a whole new dimension of love and happiness to our relationship, and she is doing very well with it, too. In just over six months of this, my life has completely turned around. I am relaxed, confident, prosperous, effective, and deliriously happy. My marriage is like a perpetual honeymoon, and I bounce out of bed every morning looking forward to another enjoyable and effective day. Al, tell everybody how wonderful it is!"

J.S. gave us this report: "I guess you would have called me a hausfrau. I honestly felt like something less than a person. Boredom is the most straightforward reason I can give you for starting my work with Isis and the super sensory perception. But I found snuggling up in Isis' lap to be quite a stimulating experience. She quickly showed me that my boredom was my own fault and helped me launch a program of becoming a whole being (I wanted to say again, but really I had never been one). There was no big hurry, so I could go along with a program of steady, sure growth. Now, after a year, I'm deeply involved in political activity and community service, from a solid base of financial independence. That came from a hobby that Isis and company showed me how to make income-producing. Believe it or not, I'm taking better care of my husband and children now than before while making better than a thousand dollars a month from my business and enjoying every waking moment. There is a wonderful new adult relationship with my husband, too. But best of all I have a solid respect for myself and know that I am a real person."

LUNAR SUPER SENSORY KINETICS—HOW TO STAY AT A PEAK OF PSYCHIC SENSITIVITY AND EFFECTIVENESS INDEFINITELY

We want to stress the idea of letting the Force work through you in all manner of helpful ways. The secret is staying loose—relaxed and aware of the subtle promptings that warn of danger and point to opportunity. I carefully called this super sensory perception because it is more than simple ESP or psychic ability. This is living, working and feeling in tune with Mother Isis as the Force, and enjoying the super effectiveness and good luck that is its natural consequence.

The ritual work we have given you in this chapter will certainly bring you initial contacts with the Force. But it will grow in usefulness and power for you only if you use it regularly and keep your approach in harmony with the positive, motherly instincts of Isis. Think of Isis in this sense as a devoted and loving mother who wants for you, her child, all possible success, growth, achievement, love, happiness and the other good things of life. But, like the good mother that she is, she also wants you to attain these wonderful things in keeping with the highest standards of ethics and consideration for others. She accepts you as you are, and always tries to gloss over your shortcomings while she encourages you to overcome them and realize your full potential.

In keeping with these ideas, LUNAR SUPER SENSORY KINETICS requires that you make a few simple promises to yourself, then strive to live up to them. Think of it as a simple affirmation that you make to yourself every morning and evening until you have made it a part of your very being. Let it go something like this: "I am not a clod. I am aware of the psychic atmosphere around me as well as the feelings and sensitivities of the people I associate with. I am in tune with Mother Isis in her role of the Force and delight in letting it work through me. Through the Force, I am completely in control of my psychic, mental, emotional and physical faculties, and my whole being-ness functions in harmony and perfect effectiveness to keep me growing spiritually, emotionally and intellectually, while piling up an ever higher mountain of significant achievements and material success. I promise Isis and myself to strive on and become ever more worthy of and in tune with the positive power we call the Force. My loving thanks to Isis and all my other spiritual associates. So mote it be."

I could give you a lot more fabulous feedback here, but it seems inappropriate. Rather, this is another point of challenge to you to earn your own results and happily eclipse anything I might write here. With the Force, everything is possible to you; let it bring you to victory after glorious victory.

MOON MAGIC MOTIVATORS

1. Super sensory perception will give you as much advantage over a normal person as he (or she) has over a blind man. It is well worth your efforts to develop it.

2. Your super sensory powers will come from attuning with Isis in her role as the Force. It will warn you of dangers in plenty of time to avoid them, alert you to opportunities of all kinds, and provide you the insight and creativity to handle any and all problems.

3. The proper way to use the Force is a turning loose or "letting" process. Let it build your definition of faith to agree with mine: *surrender to a partnership with a benevolent higher power.*

4. You have to create the contact and conditions to let the Force work through you. Begin with the MOTHER ISIS, PUT ME IN TUNE WITH THE FORCE RITE.

5. Keep the Force-triggering phrase, "Ma Ra," always in mind, and use it to make immediate emergency contact with the Force whenever you seem to be in danger or need a quick bit of special help.

6. Regular use of the SUPER SENSORY LUNAR FLOAT RITUAL will improve and maintain your contact with the Force and help you stay relaxed, prosperous and happy as you enjoy it.

7. Practice your LUNAR SUPER SENSORY KINETICS, and use the affirmation until it becomes an integral part of your very beingness.

8. Grow in all areas of your beingness in tune with the Force, and earn your own feedback that eclipses anything written here.

6

How To Use Moon Magic To Sweep All Obstacles And Limiting Conditions Out Of Your Life

We have all experienced those times when we dreamed of a divine broom sweeping through our life expression and removing or even blasting away the real or fancied obstacles to our happiness and progress. With moon magic you have a wonderful tool that will definitely do that job for you. But we must take care that we blast away only the real obstacles—indeed the fancied ones may prove to be our staunchest allies. The balancing thought here is the metaphysical classic: *Give thanks for your problems, for without them you would have no spurs to growth.*

This thing we call limitation is a powerful example. We may dream of a life that is completely free of it, but another meaning of limitation is measure. Certainly the process of measuring anything is to define its boundaries or limitations. Yet without the ability to measure, life and society as we know it would degenerate into utter chaos. The classic old TV program, "The Millionaire," did much to show us that a virtually unlimited supply of money may cause more problems than it solves. Unlimited promiscuity could produce mountains of difficulties, as would the unlimited satiation of any of our other natural appetites. Thus we see that the only effective approach is to study our situation with enough care to recognize what it is we really need, as opposed to the often harebrained changes we fancy would solve all our problems. "Seek first a deeper understanding of the situation" is our surest approach, and we now have the tools to do it well.

USING SUPER SENSORY PERCEPTION TO PINPOINT YOUR REAL OBSTACLES

How often have you heard (or thought) something like, "If only Rita were out of the picture, John would surely turn his love to me?" This sets Rita up as the obstacle to our subject's happiness and fulfillment, but it is completely erroneous. John may simply not vibrate to her at all, but all of this kind of speculation is beside the point. Our subject properly desires love and fulfillment, and the most obvious obstruction to this is her hang-up on John. With the hang-up removed, Charlie who has worshipped her from afar may get her attention and establish a mutually fulfilling relationship. All of this is by way of illustrating that we need a combination of enlightened guidance and the courage to face a momentarily unpleasant fact or two if we are to effectively work with the Force to remove the obstacles to our real growth, happiness and progress. You know better than to hand a loaded gun to an upset child. Similarly, if you are to keep a good relationship with the Force, you must never try to use it to blast willy-nilly at anything that appears to be in your way. Instead, let's learn to focus your super sensory perception on pinpointing the real obstacle. Then the proper application of the Force will assure you of positive results.

This is a time to adapt the LUNAR SUPER SENSORY FLOAT to ask for special guidance from Mother Isis. After you have nestled comfortable in Isis' lap, talk the situation over with her. Say, "Mother Isis, this is the obstacle as I believe I see it. Please give me the benefit of your wisdom and insight, and help me see beyond my own blocks and hang-ups to the truth, no matter how painful it may be for the moment." Then, just stay nestled in Isis' loving arms and be alert for any revelations that may be immediately forthcoming; but take care not to force it. If nothing seems to happen, just enjoy the love and affection and when you are ready, end the ritual as usual. Then, at those times when you are relaxed or occupied with simple routine activities, the insights will begin popping through to you. It may take a week or two for the whole picture to unfold for you, but it will be there—the trick is to recognize the truth and not fight it.

Rather than give you specific examples here, let's go on to the obstacle-removing work. Then we can let our feedback show you the whole picture.

HOW TO PREPARE FOR THE WALLS OF JERICHO OBSTACLE-SHATTERING RITUAL

First we must meet the moon in her role of Jerah, a powerful warrior goddess. Jerah usually manifests herself to us as a strong but beautiful woman in light, shining armor wearing a headdress of a silver crescent with the points up, giving the impression of horns. The biblical city of Jericho was named after her, not as a symbol of defeat but in commemoration of Joshua's glorious victory. If your memory of the story is hazy, we can refresh it enough by thinking of the words to a classic old spiritual hymn. "Joshua fit the battle of Jericho, and the walls came tumbling down." And that is the specific purpose of the ritual we are leading up to—to tumble down the walls of your obstructions and unnecessary limitations!

The most important part of your preparation was covered in our preceding section, the pinpointing of your real obstacle. You quite literally invite disaster if you use the WALLS OF JERICHO

RITUAL without being sure—think of this as the danger of knocking down the walls of your house instead of the obstruction in front of you. But, we have given you the way to handle that part, so let's begin preparing for the ritual itself. The mood should be festive, with floral incenses and perfume oils to go along with your candles. If you feel the need for precedent, review the story in your family Bible (Joshua, Chapter 6). Then comes the question, "Where do I get an army to do all that fancy marching and trumpet playing?" But that is not a problem at all; Jerah has her own army and she will delight in having it perform for you.

Finally, there is another reason for remembering the details of the story of the battle of Jericho. It is the instruction essentially to kill everybody in the city. This implies that you have reached the point where you are ready to follow through to gain a complete and total victory, paying any necessary price to make it so. There is no room for pussyfooting in battle, you must be sure you are ready allegorically to kill even all the women and children in the city. Yes, we must not take this lightly, but it is important not to enter battle full of hatred and tension, either. This is an exercise in discipline which requires a cheery attitude that can sing and fight its way to victory—fighting hard, but singing happily all the while. In this mood we are ready to start the ritual itself.

USING THE WALLS OF JERICHO RITUAL TO BRING YOUR OBSTACLES TUMBLING DOWN

Plan this as a seven-day ritual, and let nothing interfere with your doing it at some time each day for seven consecutive days. Even if you must be traveling, you can take along a small bit of incense and oil, and a couple of candles, and do your work at any old dressing table or the like. If possible, start the first ritual on the day or evening of the full moon. The next best choice is to start the day the moon reaches its perigee. We need one more mental picture to complete the preparations—picture your clearly-defined obstacle as a walled city, already under a state of siege from your mighty forces. Then at your altar, light your candles and incense, and anoint your brow, throat, heart and solar plexus with the perfume oil.

Begin the ritual itself with the MOON MAGIC AURA CLEANSING EXERCISE. When it is finished, greet Isis in the moonbeam coming to your heart and say, "Loving Mother Isis, I seek your help in your guise of Jerah, please let me see you in that form now." See the radiant form of Jerah in all her armored and crescent-horned splendor there in your special shaft of moonlight, and speak to her: "Mighty Jerah, I have clearly defined my obstacle and am certain that my spiritual, emotional, and material progress has and is being seriously impeded by its continued presence. I see it as a walled city before me, already buttoned up and under seige. I ask your help in tune with the love of the Universal Mother, Isis, in performing the ritual work to knock down the walls and destroy the city. Let the trumpets sound and the army march, now."

Then, hear the trumpets playing your favorite marching song and picture the whole host of Jerah's warriors parading once around the city. Then, thank Jerah sincerely for her help and sit in silence for a few moments to see if she has any specific guidance or instructions for you. If she does, be sure to follow through with whatever may be required of you after you have concluded the ritual. Finish as always by snuffing your candles and thanking all who may have helped.

Repeat the ritual just this way for six consecutive days (or nights). On the seventh day of the work, let the parade circle the symbolic city seven times. Then when the seventh circle is completed, join the whole host of warriors in shouting (in your imagination if necessary, but this is one of the times it helps to use your physical voice): "It is done; let the walls crumble and the city be utterly destroyed now!" And see it happen! See the walls quickly crumble to dust as the warriors sweep in and complete the destruction of everything that has held back your progress. When you feel that it is completed, thank Jerah and her army, pause to see if there is any guidance for you, then conclude the ritual normally.

RESULTS FROM THE WALLS OF JERICHO OBSTACLE SHATTERING RITUAL

D.Y. gave us this interesting report: "I was nearly five years on this job (my first one, fresh out of school), and had a few more or less cost-of-living raises, but absolutely no feeling of progress. I thought about obstacles, but I couldn't think of any, so I went to Mother Isis' lap on the moon and asked her. The two weeks went by and I swear I didn't get one bit of input on it. So I decided to play it cool and let my obstacle remain something of an oblong blur inside the walled city. This seemed to be a reasonable way to get some help without shooting up the wrong thing. I asked my spirit people to sort of fill in the blank, and I started my WALLS OF JERICHO OBSTACLE SHATTERING RITUAL that way. All I could do on the job was keep trying to do my best, then at night I enjoyed my visit with Jerah and the parade of her troops. I started on a Tuesday, so I finished the seven days of ritual the following Monday. Believe it or not, the very day after I completed the ritual, I was called to the Personnel Department. The Personnel Manager himself talked to me. He said one of the big bosses had noticed me last week and commented that I seemed far too competent to be doing my present job. This prompted a look at my records, and some red faces. I had inadvertently been left off a promotion list almost three years ago, and this had somehow left my file in something of a state of limbo. I was immediately given a double promotion and a very nice raise. My new position is both challenging and psychologically rewarding. My special thanks went to Isis, Jerah and her whole army right then. Now a special thank you to you, Al, for introducing me to the work!"

N.D. reported this experience: "I guess I'm almost one of your classic cases, Al. When I went to Isis' lap to ask about the block in my love life, I wasn't at all happy with the result. But it's true, I had been turning down dates with several very nice men because I was totally wrapped up in Joe and could think of nobody else. But Joe was literally treating me like the mud on his shoes. Reluctantly, I agreed with Isis that the WALLS OF JERICHO RITUAL should be used to destroy my obsession with him. And the more I looked at the situation objectively, the more I agreed—but part of me still longed for and would have crawled to Joe. I kept trying to be objective while waiting for the next full moon, and by the time it arrived, my intellect was quite ready to destroy the entire population of the allegorical city—even the women and children. The work with Jerah was fun, and I really enjoyed watching the parades. I started to change by the third day of the ritual work. I could tell because I began to pay extra care to my appearance all the time, and I started smiling more. The last day of the seven-day ritual was a Friday. That day, I said yes to a Saturday date with a nice gentleman I had turned down several times before; and we had a really good time! I found myself dating several very nice men before 'Mr. Right' appeared, but I met him within three months of completing the ritual. In three more months we were married; that was two weeks ago. I'm writing this after returning from our honeymoon. We are deliriously happy, as I now clearly realize I could never have been with Joe. Al, tell your people to listen to Isis and face the truth. It's truly for one's own best interest and highest good."

D.B. explained his progress this way: "I have a nice little store in a good location with plenty of passing foot traffic, but it didn't seem to be going anywhere. I tried all sorts of merchandising gimmicks and sales, but my volume stayed at something less than half what I felt it should be. The store was barely breaking even without paying me a cent, so on the personal level I was going in the hole by what it cost me to live every month. It was getting close to desperation time, so I decided I'd better try the WALLS OF JERICHO thing to see if I could break the block and get things going. When I floated up my moonbeam to sit in Mama Isis' lap, I got quite a surprise. I really heard her say that the problem was on the psychic level. Even though the building was almost new, it had a psychic atmosphere that made people ignore it, or if they came in, get a strong urge to leave. With a little reflection, I had to agree with her. I was instructed to sprinkle salt water all around the inside and outside of the store twice a day, at least until the WALLS OF JERICHO RITUAL was completed. I started with the salt the very next morning, and began the first day of the JERICHO RITUAL that night (I didn't pay any thought to timing, I needed the help now!). It was still a mediocre week, but on the seventh day of the ritual I got a feeling as if a heavy weight had been lifted from my shoulders. And sure enough, people began to drop in, mostly to browse at first, but business was up a good 10 percent above a normal week for the first 7 days after the ritual. And it went up better than 10 percent more the next week, and the next, and the next! Naturally I was smiling more by now and I'm sure that helped the atmosphere, too. Now I'm in the process of opening a second store with the extra profits from the first one. Quite a turn around! You can be sure I've thanked Isis, Jerah & Co. right along. Now another thank you, Al, for the data and suggestions that got it all started."

And J.J. gave us this feedback: "After all sorts of tests and visits to several specialists, all the doctors told me I was in perfect health, but I had almost no energy, headaches three days out of five, and a naturally miserable disposition. Since the doctors insisted I was healthy, a health ritual didn't seem in order, and the only thing left that I could think of was the obstacle shattering bit. I followed the rules, and went to sit in Isis' lap to ask for guidance as to what should be zapped out of the way. I got a few simple dietary suggestions like less dairy products and more leafy vegetables, but I came back with the idea that most of my trouble was from a thoughtform of expecting to feel bad that had been built and nurtured over many years. So the WALLS OF JERICHO RITUAL seemed quite appropriate. I've always loved a good parade, so the trumpeters became part of a snazzy drum and bugle corps. and the daily rituals were full of goose pimples and enjoyment for me. I really shouted on the seventh night and savored watching the soldiers destroy every remnant of the negative habit thoughforms. During the pause at the end of that one, I got a suggestion for some deep breathing exercises that I started on the spot. And I'm very happy to report that I'm just full of p—and vinegar! My energy level is wonderfully high, and I haven't had even a hint of a headache for well over a month now. I waited that long to be able to give you a solid report. Thanks, all, Isis, Jerah and the whole army! It's wonderful."

LUNAR FREEDOM KINETICS—HOW TO
STAY OUT OF TRAPS AND AVOID
OBSTACLES INDEFINITELY

Our country's founding fathers left us the admonition, "Eternal vigilance is the price of liberty." This is as true on the personal level as it is in national affairs, and it should set the theme of our LUNAR FREEDOM KINETICS. We have all trapped ourselves far more than once. Just a little reflection will tell you that every time it happened, it was because your emotions (greed, infatuation, fear, insecurity) got out of hand and overruled your good judgment. My favorite line here goes: Every time you (or I) have made a major mistake, there was a haunting feeling just behind your head literally screaming "No, no, don't do that, it will get you into trouble!" And our response was always the same, "Go away, don't bother me right now. I'm busy (making this big mistake)." For example, after the dissolution of a badly mismatched marriage, the feeling is, "It must have been karma, I couldn't have been dumb enough to marry someone whose approach and appetites are so completely opposed to mine!" But in your heart you know that you married out of insecurity, sympathy, or just a capitulation to constant pressure. The hindsight is magnificent, but not all that useful except to learn from our past "horrible mistakes." Thus we can think of our LUNAR FREEDOM KINETICS as an effective method of getting our hindsight in front where it can really help us.

Much of what we need is readily available by nurturing your super sensory perception to give more strength and attention to the thing I just called a haunting feeling just behind your head. Another way to describe it is a vague sense of uneasiness, or perhaps a wee, thin voice screaming, "Danger! Danger!" But regardless of what you call it, I guarantee that the warning is there, every time you are seriously planning or thinking about an action that would be a big mistake. Now you see that there is a way in which you already have your hindsight in front; it's just a matter of training yourself to pay attention. Start the sensitization process by a few post mortems. Think back to your last few serious mistakes, and remember the sensations of uneasiness that must have preceded them. Take care that this does not degenerate into self-flagellation or the old "crying over spilt milk." The idea is to learn, not to indulge in some form of self-pity. But a few minutes of memory search will show you that you already have the power. The trick is to use it.

Promise yourself that next time you get the haunting feeling, you will face it. Treat it as a person or entity; invite it to come around in front of you and discuss the situation as two rational beings. This is usually enough to spot the emotional hang-up that was about to cause your mistake. If you don't get a feeling of release and certainty about your revised decision, a special trip to Isis' lap for her loving guidance is a must. The extra time and effort you spend in this way will pay for itself many times over in avoided misery, catastrophe and expense. Don't take this part lightly; it's like preventative medicine, a little now saves a lot later.

Let's end this chapter on a totally positive note. There is a complementary phenomenon to that uneasy or haunting feeling we've been talking about. It comes from the same place and in the same way, but its message is pure enthusiasm. There are those happy times when you encounter an idea or opportunity that is just right for you, and the super sensory reaction is instantaneous enthusiasm. It is equally important to recognize these inputs and know that the way is clear to act at once. It would be as expensive or miserable to miss a good opportunity as to jump at the wrong one. But now you know that the guiding inputs are always right there, ready to help you maximize your good while avoiding the unpleasant. Use it and keep winning!

The typical report on this part of the work reads quite like this one from G.B.: "It didn't take much thought to realize that you're right about the haunting uneasiness when I'm about to make a big mistake. The enthusiasm that says 'go' may be even more useful, and I know now that it is there with plenty of help, too. The protective part kept me from losing several thousand dollars in what turned out to be foolish investment ideas that I would no doubt have bitten for without the warning; but the one I'm most thankful for was a combination. This night I was sitting in my apartment with nothing to do when the phone rang. It was a group of good friends cooking up a spontaneous bowling party. I'm a good bowler and enjoy it, but I got the uneasy feeling, so I obeyed it, made an excuse and asked to be invited next time. As I sat there wondering why I shouldn't have gone bowling, the phone rang again. It was a couple who live up the block asking me to drop over for a drink and meet a friend of theirs. This time I got the enthusiasm from behind me, so I accepted. Honestly I wondered why, since I didn't know the people all that well, but I'm learning to follow my super sensory perception. So I combed my hair, put on a sportcoat and headed out the door. It turned out that they were playing matchmaker. If I had known, I might have avoided it even against the promptings, but I was there and the girl is lovely. It's amazing how a man who thought he was a confirmed bachelor changes his mind when he meets the right lady! We were married last week. I did warn her about my moon magic first, so of course we're doing it together now. We share everything instinctively and without friction of any kind. We've only been married a week, but I'll bet you right now that it will outlast them all—it was born of moon magic and will stay nurtured that way. Thanks to Isis and all her group of spirit people, and to you, Al for the introduction."

MOON MAGIC MOTIVATORS

1. Measure is another term for limitation, so some is necessary. Get a good understanding of your situation before you decide to break your apparent limitations.

2. Promise yourself that you will exercise the courage to face the situation honestly, then apply your logic objectively to decide what the real obstacle really is.

3. If in doubt at all, take the trip to Mother Isis' lap and talk over your problem. Face the truth as it is revealed to you, and clearly pinpoint your obstacle.

4. You may find it useful to review the Bible story of the Battle of Jericho before performing the ritual, but it's a matter of choice and not all that necessary.

5. Meet Jerah and invite her help in your seven-day WALLS OF JERICHO RITUAL. Then enjoy the fun of watching the walls of your obstacles come tumbling down.

6. Practice your LUNAR FREEDOM KINETICS and let it keep you out of traps while it leads you to happy progress. The super sensory guidance is always there to help you. Train yourself to pay attention, and you will sail along, obstacle-free forever.

7

Moon Magic For
Protection From The Evil Eye
And All Other Forms Of
Secret Or Open Psychic Attack

In our public class work at E.S.P. Lab, I have often commented that there is more voodoo practiced in Louisiana and Mississippi today than in all of Africa, with California running them a close third. And it is definitely necessary to defend ourselves against such attacks. But it's probably even more important to get rid of the effects of unconscious attacks upon you by people who have no magical techniques but are full of the venom of resentment and hatred. Never dismiss the possibility of being under psychic attack as superstition! Unless you have walked through life as the perfect patsy, and never ruffled anyone's feathers in any way, you experience some degree of psychic attack very nearly daily, and, uncountered, it can cause all manner of bad luck, misery and misfortune. Regardless of what you may have thought before, the work of this chapter is extremely important to you.

PSYCHIC ATTACK IS AS REAL TODAY AS IT WAS IN THE DAYS OF THE GREATEST SUPERSTITION, BUT EVEN MORE DANGEROUS

Before the "age of enlightenment" that we consider ourselves to be in now, people believed in leprechauns, fairies, all of the little people, witches, spells, and psychic attack. But of course they didn't believe in the presence of oxygen in the air because it hadn't been discovered yet. Fortunately for the people of the old days, oxygen didn't care whether they believed in it or not, so it continued to sustain the life of their bodies. Now our intellect has brought us this age of great reason that has discovered oxygen and debunked psychic attack along with all of the little people. And what was true of oxygen then is the same for the little people now; they couldn't care less whether we believe in them. Since they are benevolent beings, that's no problem. But there is a very real danger in not recognizing the reality of possible psychic attack—it can harm you whether you believe in it or not.

Some people shrug off the whole idea of psychic attack as suggestion. But even an uncountered suggestion can work on you through your subconscious (or as I prefer to call it, pre-conscious) beingness to bring all manner of negative experience into your life. However, the complete mechanism of psychic attack is considerably more complex. One or more negative thoughtforms (built by you or someone else, consciously or unconsciously) attaches itself to your AURA (or psychic energy field, or bio-plasmic energy field if you prefer) and works in combination with your own guilts and fears to attract all manner of mishap, bad luck, accidents, aches and pains, and even physical illness to you. To be effective, it needs only to cloud your judgment at a few critical moments; but, left to grow in power and resourcefulness it can do much, much more. We must always walk the narrow line between practical reality and paranoia when considering this very real problem. It reminds me of that famous wisecrack, "So you're paranoid, they still may be out to get you!" The meaning of this for me is simply that we must keep our balance, but when in doubt at all, some form of psychic cleansing and protection is still indicated. You might say it's better to take one shower too many than to risk stinking. It's the "same difference" here.

HOW TO SPOT THE SYMPTOMS OF
PSYCHIC ATTACK

A sudden shift in your mood toward the negative, sharp but fleeting pains, an unusual bit of clumsiness, nearly closing that big deal only to have it blow at the last minute, momentary dizziness—all of these are potential symptoms of the early stages of psychic attack. These tend to develop into fights with your friends and loved ones, serious accidents, runs of miserable luck, bad respiratory ailments, serious illness of any kind, loss of job, broken marriage, financial disaster and even death of your physical body, but no doubt after a long period of suffering.

Fortunately, this process is reversible at almost any stage. Obviously, the sooner you take corrective action, the less mess there will be to overcome, so the more energy and resources will be left for positive things. We may all dream of a world of only charm and beauty where nasty problems like these cannot exist, but the only way to get there is to earn your passage by properly handling hourself in this world just as it is. We must recognize psychic attack as like "being a little bit pregnant,"; it won't go away by being ignored; it must be faced and the problem handled in the quickest and most positive manner possible. But prevention is always the best and cheapest treatment, so we will have a go at that before we talk about ways to break the grip of an old spell.

HOW TO RECOGNIZE AND ELIMINATE
PSYCHIC ATTACK BEFORE THE SYMPTOMS
APPEAR

There are always psychic warnings of attack well before any physical symptoms appear. Clearly, to recognize and neutralize any attack before it has had time to cause physical damage is the way of least pain. There are two approaches to preventative psychic defense that are best when practiced in parallel. The first is an idea that we might call psychic hygiene. It is simply the deliberate practice of keeping your psychic atmosphere clean. As our old friend, Ralph Waldo Emerson, was so fond of saying, "All of a man is not contained between his hat and his boots." There is an energy field around your body called your AURA (or in the Russian terminology the bio-plasmic energy field) which is just as much *you* as is your physical body. And it takes just a little concentration to become aware of it. It is nice if you can actually see your AURA, and I have given many techniques for this in my previous books, but seeing it is not a requirement of being aware of it. You can see your skin by looking at it directly or in a mirror, but that is not the way you normally sense that something has touched it or penetrated it. No, you naturally say, I feel it when you touch me; and though it is a bit more subtle, you can also feel it when something touches your AURA.

A touch naturally registers with us as pleasant or unpleasant, warm and friendly, or rough and hostile—and you can often tell by the feel that it is a special loved one who is touching you. The technique of extending this beyond the physical confines of your skin is to imagine once more; this time, to imagine that your sense of feeling extends say 6 inches out all around your body. Then try to be aware of the feelings at the new sensory perimeter. And if you feel anything uncomfortable or vaguely threatening, take the necessary action to remove it from your presence. We will discuss that in our next section. Meanwhile, consider also that the 6-inch boundary can soon be extended to 2 or 3 feet, thus giving you the full sensory command of your personal psychic atmosphere. This practice will not only serve to help you stay out of trouble, but will also prove a recognition device for creative ideas that may hang around you in hopes of being noticed. Practice will indeed pay you big dividends!

But what shall you do for knowledge of your psychic atmosphere while you are striving to perfect your new auric sensitivity? This is the program which I suggested should run in parallel with the first. Let's call it the MOTHER ISIS, SHOW ME THE CONDITION OF MY AURA RITE. It is best to do this just after your morning and evening MOON MAGIC AURA CLEANSING EXERCISE. With your bright moon still pictured in front of you, ask: "Mother Isis, please show me the condition of my AURA, including any potential threats to my overall well-being." The answering picture may be just fields of color, or it may show you a picture of an attacking entity or thoughform. Obviously if you see something unwholesome, psychic defense measures are indicated. Also, if you see only colors, all is well if they are bright and clear. The absence of a color is fine also, but if one or more of the colors you see is dull or muddy, it indicates a weakness or blockage in its corresponding chakra which requires more chakra cleansing work. For those of you who are not familiar with color/chakra relationship it is as follows: red for the root, orange for the spleen, yellow for the solar plexus, green for the heart, blue for the throat, indigo for the brow, and violet for the crown chakra.

A POWERFUL MOON-MIRROR RITE FOR DEFEATING OR REVERSING PSYCHIC ATTACK

I personally prefer to harness the energy of psychic attack and make it do something helpful for me. But at first, the best way is simply to become a mirror and reflect the attack back to its originator. It's easy to think of this in terms of being like the moon itself, reflecting away those energies you do not need, but always first extracting anything that can be safely used for your good. From the viewpoint of earth, the moon seems to keep virtually all the energy for herself at new moon times, then give it all to us at full moon time. Similarly, you will at first be like a full moon, reflecting away all the energy of the attack, but as you become more accomplished as a moon magician, you will keep more and more of the energy to help you further your own positive projects. The purpose of our MOON-MIRROR RITE is to set you up as a full reflector of any negative energy or attack thoughform that may come your way. Next we will give you the technique for adjusting the amount reflected to just the part you can't yet use positively.

White candles for your altar, and sandalwood, jasmine or protection oil and incense should be used. Anoint at least your brow, throat, heart and solar plexus chakras with the oil, light your candles and incense, and begin the MOON MAGIC AURA CLEANSING EXERCISE. Then, with that gorgeous shaft of moonlight flowing straight to your heart, address Isis: "Lovely Mother Isis, I seek your special help in protecting myself from all forms of psychic attack. Please help me build a sphere of light around me which will reflect away all attacking energy that I cannot harness for my good. Help me become a model of your symbol, the moon, able to reflect or repel with ease any spell, attack or negative energy that may come my way."

Picture your shaft of moonlight forming into a shimmering ball about three feet out from your body and completely engulfing you. Know that it is sensitive to your AURA and will move with you wherever you go. It is solid outside, but easily penetrated from inside; to send out resentment, jealousy or any of the negative emotions is to poke huge holes in your sphere of protection. This gives us a fresh and powerful reason for striving to live a completely positive life, but because none of us is perfect, it's also a reason to renew your protection regularly. OK, you've built your protective sphere of LIGHT, now let's activate it. This is another job for the Force as we met it in Chapter 5. To put yourself in tune with the Force as it is to act through you, we use the phrase, "Ma Ra." Therefore, to turn on the Force as the activator of your psychic defense mechanism, we use the reverse phrase, "Ra Ma." This completes your basic system of active and passive use of the Force. "Ma Ra" turns on the Force to act through you, while "Ra Ma" sets the Force as the invincible power of your psychic protection. And the more you use it, the stronger it gets in its ability to work through and for you.

Affirm the connection to Isis. Speak: "Thank you, Mother Isis, for the gift of the dual connection to your power as the Force. I will speak the Ma Ra to put myself in the hands of the Force to act through me, and Ra Ma to activate my invincible psychic protection. I will strive to the best of my ability to stay positive in attitude and action that I may forever be worthy of your love and help. Again, my loving thanks to you for this wonderful power to move ever more creatively and happily through this earthly life." Then, snuff your candles and the rite is completed. You may repeat the rite whenever you feel the need to renew your contact, but constant use will keep it powerful and alive also.

WHAT TO EXPECT FROM THE APPLICATION OF YOUR MOON-MIRROR PROTECTIVE POWER

Roger S. gave us this report on the use of the rites: "All of a sudden my highly successful business started turning sour. There were unbelievable foul-ups, merchandise returns and lost customers where there had been only efficiency and satisfaction before. My young son came down with a malady the doctors couldn't explain, and my loving wife turned into something closely resembling a shrew. I turned quickly to Isis for help, asking for a vision to show me what was wrong. She showed me a hideous picture of a secretary I had recently let go because she was incapable of doing her work. I have never before seen such a look of pure venom and hatred. So I built three separate spheres of protective light, one for me, one for my family, and another for my business. I charged it all up with the Ra Ma, and regularly used the Ma Ra on my way to work, seeking the guidance and effectiveness to clean up my whole operation. My boy bounced back to radiant health in less than 36 hours, and with that pressure off, my wife began to loosen up. As the Force, I pulled off several minor miracles in the business—saved all of the lost customers and got everything running smoothly, and business growing again! The Ma Ra/Ra Ma combination had it all cleaned up and better than ever in less than two weeks. Incidentally, I heard later that just about the time I got things smoothed out, the ex-secretary was hospitalized with a nervous breakdown. I was sorry to hear that and wish her well. I particularly wish for her that she learns enough about herself not to get back into this sort of mess again. Thanks, Isis, Al, and all!"

Sally B. had this happy result: "By my 27th birthday, I decided there must be some sort of curse on me. I started dating when I was 15, and in the whole 12 years since, I had never been out with the same man more than 4 or 5 times. I'm not at all unattractive, and never had any problem in attracting the attention of desirable males. But something always seemed to make one or both of us lose interest. So I gave myself a special birthday present, a trip to see Isis. She showed me a time when I was still in my mother's womb. An unmarred aunt who was insanely jealous of my mother (I think she lost out in the competition for my father) cursed her during the pregnancy. The effect was that my mother could have no more children (I'm an only child), and I was never to marry or even have a steady boy friend. The prescription from Isis was a double whammy, a combination of the WALLS OF JERICHO RITUAL and the MOON-MIRROR RITE. We needed the MOON-MIRROR protection to be able to do an effective breaking of the old block that had indeed solidified into a wall. And I'm very happy to say it worked perfectly. It was worth the years of waiting! The really ideal man found me. We dated for three months before we decided to see how it would be to live together. In just three more months we were both sure, and we were married last week. I guarantee you it's a happy one. Thanks to Isis and all!"

THE LUNAR FLOAT ME ABOVE ALL
DANGER AND NEGATIVITY RITE

We spoke of reprogramming the energy of attacking thoughforms and the like to make them work for your progress instead of against you. That is the purpose of the FLOAT ME ABOVE ALL DANGER AND NEGATIVITY RITE. First recognize that energy of itself is neutral, it is neither positive nor negative until it is programmed. The classic example is electricity—it is energy that doesn't know or care whether it is used to light your room, cook your dinner, or kill a man in the electric chair. As you learn to float above the level of any programmed attack, you have the opportunity to compltely change its programming and so cause it to work powerfully positive magic for your benefit. But this is safe only when you are sure that you are floating securely above the negativity. The approach should be plenty of enjoyable practice of the FLOATING RITE before you dabble with the reprogramming of the energy.

This rite uses the same candles, incense and perfume oil as for the MOON-MIRROR PROTECTION work. In fact it is best used as an extension or follow-up to the MOON-MIRROR RITE, but it doesn't necessarily have to be done on the same day or at the same time. If you are doing it as an immediate follow-up, skip the MOON MAGIC AURA CLEANSING EXERCISE because you have just done it. Either way, the next step is to return to that beautiful shaft of moonlight coming to your heart, and again speak to Isis: "Now, Mother Isis, with your help I will acquire the power to float above all attack and easily reprogram it to accomplish good in my life. I understand that the process is one of spiritual orientation and attunement to literally change the rate of vibration of my AURA and that of my possessions and affairs such that we are collectively so far above the mundane world that all of its negativity is safely far below us. I will use the key words 'Spiritual Float' to trigger the process this time, and whenever I need it in the future. Let's try it now. Thank you. Spiritual Float."

Then feel your sphere of light floating up with you in it, but this "up" is into the higher spiritual realms. From this vantage point, you can look "down" on the psychic sea below you and clearly see the negative or attacking thoughtforms. Note that a thoughtform looks rather like an egg or a big single cell, with the programming at the place of the yolk or nucleus. Negative programming will appear as a dark, muddy nucleus, while a positive nucleus is bright and sparkling. All you need do to put a stray thoughtform to work for you is to send a shaft of sparkling blue light from your throat chakra to its nucleus to break it up. Then quickly follow with a ray of indigo light from your brow chakra along which you project a bright picture of the new, positive goal for the thoughtform. See your picture form, then bathe it with green light, love and enthusiasm from your heart chakra to permanently reset the nucleus. When you know it is finished, look around at the rest of your psychic atmosphere to be sure it is clean and clear. Reprogram any other negative thoughtforms. Then, when all is beauty around you, settle back down into full contact with your body and environment, and enjoy the peace along with the extra help from the changed thoughtforms.

This is another of those areas that will continue to improve for you just as long as you keep using it. And a little reflection on the technique will prove to you that this is the perfect way to drive your enemies to abject frustration—every time they take a shot at you, they soon see that it has helped your progress in some wonderful way. Thus, if they are smart, they will leave you alone. But, if they are stupid enough to keep trying, they keep helping you by supplying the energy to power your super helpful thoughtforms.

I looked at my feedback for this section, but it reads too much like pure science fiction to print here. Let's let it blend in quietly with the results of the LUNAR PROTECTION KINETICS that we will present to you next.

LUNAR PERFECT PROTECTION KINETICS

This is what we might call the balance to the natural desire for fame and fortune. The requirement for never being the object of psychic attack is a low profile which attracts no notice and so no jealousy, combined with a program of going out of your way never to offend anyone or ruffle any feathers. Obviously, nobody would want to live that way, which is the reason we gave you the defense and thoughtform reprogramming techniques first. But

LUNAR KINETICS requires that you recognize the probability of generating extra psychic attack, and take it into account as one factor in your decision to take or refrain from any action. The result of good judgment in this area is to avoid a few actions that are really unimportant to you but that would stir up a disproportionate amount of resentment or antagonism in someone else—with a much more peaceful and effective life for both of you as a reward. I won't overwork this point, but a wise moon magician will certainly take it to heart.

Let's share one typical report on this part of the work. This one is from Sharon S.: "After a bitter divorce, J and I continued to fight over all manner of little things about the children. I was pretty miserable and had the terrible feeling of being boxed in and not able to get ahead in any way. Then I tried a combination of the thoughtform reprogramming to get rid of the accumulated resentment of both of us, and some sensible LUNAR PROTEC-TION KINETICS. I promised myself to be more flexible about J's visits with the children, to have them ready on time, and to be pleasant about the whole situation. I reprogrammed the negative thoughtforms to get me a raise and a promotion at work—that seemed like the best way to use up the old energy—and I really worked at being nice instead of spiteful to J. The first happy result I noticed was in my kids. They started to be nicer and more cooperative to me. Next, J handed me an extra check for two hundred dollars, saying he had had a bit of good luck he wanted to share with me and the kids. Within 6 weeks I got my promotion and raise along with some nice compliments on my work and my improving attitude toward everything. Then came the capper. J brought the children home rather late one Sunday night and asked if he could help me put them to bed. When they were safely tucked away, I offered J a cup of coffee. As we chatted, he told me how much he appreciated my new mature attitude and how with me acting this way he strongly wished we had never parted. Suddenly we found ourselves making love more passionately than even on our honeymoon. We were remarried last week after agreeing that we can function together as mature adults, and we both feel that all the old negativity is gone. The kids are ecstatic—we are a really happy family for the first time!"

MOON MAGIC MOTIVATORS

1. Psychic attack can hurt you whether you believe in it or not. In fact, it is more dangerous to the nonbeliever because it then works without opposition.

2. Psychic attack is much more than suggestion, but even an uncountered suggestion can be harmful to you.

3. Review the symptoms of psychic attack and stay alert to notice them so you can adopt defensive measures before any attack has time to do you serious harm.

4. The best defense is to spot attack before the physical symptoms appear. Check your AURA and the thoughtforms 2 or 3 feet around you and regularly. When you sense any form of hostility, take defensive action.

5. Build your MOON MIRROR SPHERE OF LIGHT and wear it always. Activate it for defense by calling on the Force with the Ra Ma phrase. Remember, it's "Ma Ra" for the Force in action, and "Ra Ma" to set your defenses.

6. Use the LUNAR FLOAT RITE and learn to float above all attack and reprogram the thoughtforms to make them work for you instead of against you.

7. Practice your LUNAR PROTECTION KINETICS along with your psychic defense, and reprogramming of thoughtforms to lead a "charmed life" forevermore.

8

Moon Magic,
The Key To Fulfilling
Your True Destiny

When we turn to the problem of personal destiny, I'm reminded of a classic line from the old song, "Custer's Last Stand." It's a plaintive, "What am I doing here?" Certainly we all have times when we feel that way, and if we don't get maudlin about it, they are good for us. Once in a while it is necessary to seriously question your purpose for being here in a physical body, and not settle for a cartoon type answer like "mashed potatoes." There really is a meaningful answer for you, let's set about finding it.

DO YOU HAVE A SPECIAL, PERSONAL
MISSION IN THIS LIFE?

Because of the grave danger of launching you on a wild ego
trip, I tried to set a mood of levity, bordering on the flip, with our
opening paragraph. Yes, you certainly do have a special and
personal mission in this physical body, but it must be kept in
careful perspective—otherwise, it will flip you so far out of
balance that failure becomes almost inevitable. Thus, our first
task is to prepare you to see and comprehend your mission while
carefully keeping both feet on a solid foundation of true prac-
ticality. About here, you may wonder what all the caution and
fuss is about. So, let's lay it out as simply and directly as the
language permits. The danger is that you will see your mission
clearly and become so enthusiastic or overwhelmed that you will
drop everything in your attempt to immediately fulfill it. The
resultant shirking of your financial and other mundane responsibilities will all too often sink your whole ship and set you back
many years or even lifetimes on your path of balanced growth
and accomplishment.

Thus, the first step in preparation is to set a better perspective. It begins by considering the classic apparent conflict between
fate or determinism and free will. How can there be free will if you
have a predetermined mission? Those of you who know me well
will recognize a classic Zen paradox in the question, and realize at
once that there must be a higher truth that resolves it. This time
the higher truth is derived from the perspective of more than one
lifetime on earth. In Chapter 11, we will go deeply into your past
lives, but for now it is only necessary to imagine the planning
process prior to your physical birth. At that time, you exercised
your free will to accept a set of major goals to be accomplished
during this particular earthly sojurn. And it is quite like signing a
legal contract down here—you are bound by your word, even
though it was given prior to entry into this physical body. Some
people come into this life with very few commitments, while
others bring so many that they seem totally bound up in
obligations with almost no room for the luxury of immediate

choice. But we see the same thing in earth life itself—some get all bound up in multiple alimony problems, or just a bunch of debts from unwise spending or gambling, while others remain quite unfettered.

On the personal level, my early life seemed quite restricted. There was a tremendous amount of this thing we call drive, but every time I tried a path that might lead me away from what has become the work of E.S.P. Laboratory, I got quickly knocked flat on my backside! Also, a goodly portion of the overall picture was withheld from me for a long time, and in retrospect, rightfully, too. If I had clearly seen how much work I was letting myself in for, I might very well have "chickened out" and tried to remain in some comfortable business executive position. But all worked out well because I was able to get enough information to get me headed in the right direction, and that is what we want to do for you.

The rest of your preparation is easy, but it requires a definite commitment of willpower. It is simply to promise yourself that, regardless of what you see for your mission (or missions) in life, you will continue to fulfill all of your present commitments and obligations while you maneuver for position to begin serious work on your pre-birth accepted assignments.

THE MOTHER ISIS, SHOW ME MY DESTINY INCANTATION AND RITUAL

Setting the mood for this inquiry is the key to getting accurate and meaningful results. Part of this involves recognition of the practical meaning of what the Eastern philosophies call karma. Karma is the working out of problems and obligations not resolved in past lives, and it plays an important part in the pre-birth planning process. It's not always possible to handle the whole accumulation in one life and have time left for evolution and growth, too, but with the wisdom of many lifetimes you have right then, you agree to an ambitious but workable life plan. Thus, the mood we seek is one of wise contemplation of your

pre-accepted goals, in the company of congenial and understanding friends. Add to this the understanding that for your own
good you may not be permitted to see the whole picture at one
time, and we are ready to start the ritual.

This is a time for candles, your favorite floral incense, and
perfume oil. Light your candles and incense, anoint your brow,
throat, heart and solar plexus chakras with the oil, and begin with
the MOON MAGIC AURA CLEANSING EXERCISE. Then, with
the beautiful shaft of moonlight coming to your heart, speak to
Isis, "Mother Isis, I long to better understand the special purposes
for my being here in this body and life. Please take me and my
band of spirit guides and helpers with you to your lovely home on
the moon and help them show me the plan I agreed to for this
life. I know that I may not be permitted to see the whole thing at
once, but there is surely enough that I may better understand
how I fit into the scheme of things. Thank you for your wonderful
help." Now let yourself float gently up the moonbeam in the
company of your spirit band (we'll meet them on a more
personal and intimate level in our next chapter), and settle down
comfortably beside the loving figure of Isis. Feel the other
interested, friendly presences as you relive the decision/contract-
making portion of your pre-birth time. Let the picture of the time,
shortly before your birth into this present body, when you saw,
understood and agreed to your life goals and assignments,
unfold easily before you.

This part is widely different from individual to individual.
You may see yourself in the body of your immediate past life, in
earnest conference with a group of people you will come to
recognize as your spirit band—or everything you get may be
completely abstract and apparently impersonal—or anything in
between! Either way, the secret to making the ritual effective and
useful for you is to simply let it unfold as much information as
possible for you, soak it up in your current memory banks, then
later ask each memory for its practical importance and usefulness
to you. You may get what seems to be almost a full-length movie,
or just one or two fleeting impressions. But, whatever comes has
a definite bearing on your present situation, and letting it help
explain your "now" will actually give you a better set of handles

on it, and therefore on your future. Don't press, and don't hold out for a whole panorama of startling pictures and information. Just accept what comes, and know that you will remember it for contemplation later. If there is any doubt about remembering, be sure you take along pencil and paper and make notes before you close your ritual. If you don't seem to get very much, you know that you can repeat the ritual as often as you'd like, so just enjoy the feeling of good fellowship, and be alert to bring back even the slightest clues to your prearranged goals. When you feel that you have remembered as much as you are going to, thank Isis and your spirit band, settle gently back into your body, and conclude the ritual by snuffing your candles.

WHAT THE SHOW ME MY DESTINY RITUAL HAS BROUGHT TO OTHERS

Let me begin this discussion by completing the personal note I started in our opening section. I spent many years in industry in positions of controller, financial vice president, executive vice president, and even president of successful and growing companies. Outwardly I was a big success, almost a boy wonder, but through it all I was restless and generally dissatisfied. There was an instinctive drive to use the mails to further my career. I was constantly buying reams of fresh resumés and mailing them in answer to virtually every position offered in the classified section of both major Los Angeles newspapers and the Wall St. Journal. And though that never seemed to bear fruit, this only intensified the drive. Then at long last, I saw the blueprint for E.S.P. Laboratory that I had agreed to before entering this body, and I understood! So I started the lab with a mailing of just 100 pieces of introductory literature—and got an unheard of 30 positive responses! And we have grown mightily ever since, because I finally realized that the drive to the mails was my pre-birth agreement to find a way to help people who can't or simply are not particularly inclined to go out of the house for their psychic/spiritual guidance and help. I have been as fulfilled in my work through E.S.P. Lab as I was frustrated in my work in industry. Just a brief glimpse at the pre-birth goal setting process brought me that tremendous amount of both help and relief from the psychic pressures—and it can do the same or more for you!

H.T. sent us this report: "I am a very successful business-man, but I was suffering from an uncomfortable degree of restlessness, so I decided to try your ISIS, SHOW ME MY GOALS RITUAL. And was I surprised at what it showed me! It was an agreement to take plenty of extra trouble to make a man out of a rather delicate soul I recognized as my son. In all honesty, he was so sickly as a young child that I subconsciously avoided him by devoting all of my energies to my work. But now I had the material success, so there was no excuse to shirk my agreed-upon responsibility. I promised myself to delegate authority better and spend more time with my son. The timing was magnificent! (Thanks, I'm sure to plenty of prodding from spirit.) I bought a football and helmet and shoulder pads for the boy, and started to play with him. He's small, but quick and very dedicated. After only about a year, the kid went out for high school football, and made first string halfback. The team calls him "The Feather" because he's so tiny, but he has their respect and is a good little scatback. My family life is happy and rewarding. My wife has responded wonderfully, and I know that my boy is becoming a real man. It's amazing, Al, by accepting my pre-birth agreement, I also got the balance I so badly needed in my own life! Thanks to you, and the wonderful spirit people who prodded me into my new happiness!"

M.D. reported this way: "I was in my second year of nursing school, when suddenly I seemed to turn sour on the whole bit. Fortunately I had been dabbling in your moon magic, so I figured a look at my pre-birth agreements was immediately necessary. There on the moon in that lovely company, I saw an agreement to be the inspiration and love influence behind a young man I recognized. D. and I sort of grew up as childhood sweethearts, but I had never really taken him seriously as we grew older. Through it all he never gave up; he still called me at least once a month to ask for a date, even though it had been over two years since I had accepted him. By 'coincidence' he called me the next day and I agreed to go to a dance with him, at the expense of cutting a very important class. On the date I looked at him in a new light, of course, and we had a marvelous time. That weekend, he asked me to quit nursing school and marry him. I said yes, without any hesitation, and we were married the following weekend. We only had a couple of days for our honeymoon, but it was delightful. Now we're back and I'm happily fulfilling my pre-birth agreement. Al, it's wonderful! I didn't think it possible to be this happy!"

HOW TO HANDLE YOUR MAJOR PRE-BIRTH ASSIGNMENTS

First let's answer the logical question, "What do you do if you don't seem to get any pictures or other inputs about pre-birth agreements?" I guarantee you that a continued feeling of restlessness means that there is something you're supposed to be doing. So repeat the ritual about twice a week, and each time, if you seem to get no immediate response, invite Isis and your spirit friends to give you the needed information in a dream or any way they can get it to you. Then stay alert to recognize the information that will lead you to positvely solve your restlessness.

On the other hand, what do you do if you get assignments that seem completely impossible to you? We'll get you lots more help on this in our next chapter, but for now, let's apply the practical principles of idea manifestation. Regardless of its magnitude, anything you agreed to accomplish in the pre-birth planning period brings with it its own means of manifestation. Your part is to recognize the assignment and cooperate with it as if it were a living entity itself, which in a very practical sense it is. Are you too proud to talk with an idea? That would cost you far more than you should be prepared to pay. The technique can be as simple or as complicated as you like, but the essential part is to contemplate the assignment or idea, decide that you really want it to come to pass, then enthusiastically ask it, "How can I help you come into full manifestation?" Of course, it's necessary to be quiet enough to notice the answer, and since you are conversing with an idea, you wouldn't expect to hear a voice responding. An idea communicates by projecting an *idea*. If you stay relaxed and reasonably detached, you can carry on quite an extended conversation and get the outline of even a complicated plan of achievement—you ask your question aloud, and accept the answer as a responding idea that seems to "pop" into your head.

Then it's up to you to apply your logic and good judgment to develop a detailed plan with an attainable set of sub-goals and a realistic timetable for their accomplishment. In my *Helping Yourself with Psycho-Cosmic Power* (which is now unfortunately out of print) I went into great detail with a "pert chart" approach. Let's simplify it here by saying that you list all the things that have to be accomplished to reach a given goal or sub-goal, with the time it takes to do each one. Then do as much as you can on the one that takes the longest, then the next longest and so on just like planning to bring a dinner to the table with all the dishes hot and at a peak of flavor and nourishment all at the same time. Most people handle their short-run tasks this way instinctively, so it should be a relatively easy thing for you to extend the same thinking to your major goals.

PROGRESS COMES ONLY FROM EFFECTIVENESS IN THE "NOW"

The goal/sub-goal planning and scheduling idea leads us to the real secret of any long-range success. It must be "effectiveness in the now!" I invariably think of a massive project like the building of the Great Wall of China in this regard. It took many man-years of hard labor with what we would consider extremely primitive equipment, but because it was planned carefully and executed with diligence, it stands today as a monument to the potential for human achievement. For most of us, relative to the building of China's Great Wall, our tasks are uncomplicated with few of the really major logistics problems. But they are still best completed in the same way, by sufficient effectiveness in the "now" to keep piling up a series of small achievements until they become a truly major accomplishment. The trick is wise planning combined with perseverance; if you vacillate or keep changing

your mind and redoing the same thing, you'll never get anywhere. But, even when you feel you don't understand very much
of the overall picture, you can still ask yourself, "Is there
something I'm sure has to be done, regardless of possible shifts in
the long-term direction?" Then get an answer and perform the
task, so you can move on to the next one, and you will be
developing a habit of effectiveness that will carry you to eventual
victory while it establishes in you all the strength it takes to keep
winning indefinitely.

Because of the period covered and the potential involved,
feedback on this section would have to be so completely
disguised as to make it useless—otherwise, the highly successful
lives would be so obvious that there is no way to protect the big
winners' anonymity. So, instead of lesser or disguised examples,
let's challenge you to set your own course from waiting on tables
(or whatever you happen to be doing at the moment) to the
Governor's Mansion, the White House, the corporate board
chairmanship of your choice, or even a Nobel Prize. Nothing is
impossible to you with just what you have learned so far! And we
have much more power and help to unfold for you in chapters
yet to come. Let's strive on together and produce a really super
winner, *you*!

LUNAR FULFILL MY DESTINY KINETICS

Before we turn to enlisting an army of spirit people to help
you, let's wrap up this chapter with a discussion of its LUNAR
KINETICS. First comes the question, "How do I know when I
have fulfilled my spiritual mission?" And the stock answer is, "As
long as you are still inhabiting your physical body, your mission is
not complete." In one very real sense that answer is totally true.
You are involved with your personal evolutionary process from
the day of your birth until the day you permanently vacate the
physical body. But it is also quite possible to fulfill all of your pre-
birth contracts and have the remaining portion of your life to
launch new projects more completely in tune with the interests
and tastes of your personality as you have evolved it in this

present earthly sojourn. As always, we bump into another question, "How do I know when all of my pre-birth agreements have been fulfilled?" There are two steps here that should share equal importance.

First, you should notice that all of the old restlessness has been replaced by a happy sense of accomplishment and contentment. Take care that this is not just a disguise for the old bugaboo of complacency that could lead you to sit on your haunches and invite disaster. But, complacency aside, we know that any restlessness almost invariably means you have more pre-birth agreements to finish. Now let's assume that you have completed the first step and honestly feel that you are free to follow your interests or whims. The second step is something of a courtesy call on Isis to be sure. Prepare for one more MOTHER ISIS, SHOW ME MY DESTINY RITUAL, but this time approach it with, "Mother Isis, I feel that I have completed all of my pre-birth assignments and agreements, but I want your confirmation. Please let me join you and my spirit band on your beautiful moon that I may hear if you agree. And if you do agree, I am still open to your guidance as to how I may best use the balance of this lifetime on earth." Then enjoy your happy float to the moon, and again pay careful attention to what your friends have to say.

Most people are in their late 50's or into their 60's before their pre-birth agreements are completed, but there is plenty of variance from one individual to another. Just remember that it's not true until Isis and your spirit band agree, but when they do, complete control of the balance of your life reverts to you as you know yourself now! And you may experience something of a reward for a job well done.

RESULTS OF LUNAR FULFILL MY DESTINY KINETICS

Abner S. gave us this report: "Right after my retirement party, I rather expected to sit quietly on my front porch and peacefully smoke my pipe, at least for a few months. After 47 years of work, I felt I must have fulfilled all my obligations, but I had the time now, so I took your advice and made the courtesy call on Isis. And was I surprised! The assignments were not over. I was shown an agreement to help a man I recognized, but would never have thought of as needing help. He's, shall we say, way above me on the economic ladder, but his business was running into serious trouble. I was also reminded of a process I had often used in a somewhat complicated hobby of mine, and I realized it would be a natural in his business. I wasn't sure I knew him well enough to call him, but I tried and it worked. When we sat down to talk, I simply told him that now that I had some spare time I had been thinking about how my old hobby process might fit into his operation. He was ecstatic! And he asked me if I would come in as a consultant for a year to get things going properly. The year's fee was a full five times my highest earnings in the past. The job was more fun than work, and it did solve his production cost problems. Now I'm off on a world cruise I never thought I could afford—and with the blessings of Isis and my spirit friends because I'm now free to indulge in a few pet whims. Thanks again for suggesting that courtesy call on Isis. It was rewarding for many people!"

Shirley G. reported this experience: "I was a dutiful wife for all those years, but I never felt my husband really loved me. Anyway, the kids were long since married and gone, and after my husband's funeral I was thinking about some extensive traveling. But I felt I should follow directions and check with Isis for any remaining pre-birth agreements. Honestly, I figured that when Carl passed over all my pre-planned obligations were finished, but Isis and my spirit people seemed to have other ideas. I was shown a picture of a man I didn't recognize, and with it came the feeling that I was to make his later life especially happy. I wondered if I had just let my imagination run wild, and I more or less forgot about it, but I hesitated about making any final decisions on an extended trip. Just 10 days after the moon session, a friend called and said she had someone she wanted me to meet. Would anyone believe that for two over-50 people it was love at first sight? It was the man I saw in the picture on the moon. I'm writing this just before leaving on my extended trip, but now I won't be alone. We were married last week—and this is at last an 'obligation' I'm enthralled about fulfilling!"

MOON MAGIC MOTIVATORS

1. In considering the subject of your life mission, it is important to avoid either an ego trip or excessive enthusiasm for the assignment to the neglect of your normal life responsibilities.

2. Recognize that a pre-birth agreement or acceptance of an assignment is not a negation of your free will, but an example of exercise of your free will by the more complete being you were immediately before your physical birth.

3. Restlessness is a sure sign that you should be working on a pre-birth assignment. Use the MOTHER ISIS, SHOW ME MY DESTINY RITUAL to find out what it is.

4. You may not be permitted to see your whole life picture at once, but you are always entitled to see the immediate cause of your restlessness. Repeat the ritual once or twice a week until you have enough good information to make a positive start on the assignment that is causing your restlessness.

5. Major pre-birth assignments require careful planning to insure your successful accomplishment. Talk it over with the idea, asking it how you can best help it manifest. Let it help you lay out a plan with many sub-goals and a timetable for their completion. Then take one positive step at a time to certain victory.

6. Effectiveness in the "now" is the secret of carrying your plans to successful completion . Study the basic principles given in this section and you will become a super achiever.

7. LUNAR DESTINY KINETICS require regular checking with Isis and your spirit band, particularly if you feel that all your pre-birth assignments are completed. Often, there is one more that can prove especially rewarding.

Moon Magic, Destiny And Your Spirit Helpers

A very real part of your mission in this physical body is to become a master of the psychic energies in your own right and thus be master of your environment and future. So I waited until now to seriously bring up the subject of your spirit guides and helpers. By this point in our study you have learned the secrets of working with the psychic energies and their related universal personalities, so you have earned the deeper contact and extra cooperation of your own group of spirit beings. First lets be sure that you understand the mutually rewarding reasons for getting a closer working relationship with your band of spirit friends and helpers.

WHY WE ALL NEED OUR SPIRIT HELPERS

For those of you who are not fully familiar with the joys and advantages of spirit contact, lets think of a practical, physical analogy. In our normal daily life there is plenty of interrelationship with other human beings, and we recognize the ability to communicate with one another as an essential part of being comfortable and effective in the material world. We look upon a person who is deaf or blind as having a major handicap. And one who is totally deaf and blind finds it quite impossible to function in anything like a normal manner. The family (or the state) must take care of such a person with great diligence or he will surely perish. We humans do not live in a spiritual/psychic vacuum. We are spiritual and psychic beings just as surely as we are physical beings. Now think about this: from the time of birth into your present physical body, you have been cared for by your "family" of spirit helpers, because you were essentially deaf and blind in that sphere of your life. Imagine the joy and relief to a material family when their member who has been so totally handicapped finally begins to regain even partial use of these faculties! You have arrived at a point where you can bring much the same mixture of joy and relief to your dedicated family of spirit helpers as you learn to recognize their presence, and work to take over some of the basic responsibilities for your psychic and spiritual functioning.

From this you should see clearly why you need your band of spirit helpers. Up until recently, they have been totally in charge of your spiritual/psychic existence, though largely without your knowledge. Anyway, you have relied completely upon them for your protection, nourishment, hygiene and inspiration on all but the grossest material levels. Just as one never completely outgrows his family, you will always enjoy your spirit band. But now it is time for you to recognize their presence and help, and begin to cooperate with them in your progress, until you finally reach the stage where you are as helpful (or even more so) to them as they are to you. This is an integral part of your personal mission for this lifetime, and now is the best time to set about beginning the get acquainted process.

HOW TO LET THE LOVE GODDESS, DIANA, INTRODUCE YOU TO YOUR SPIRIT BAND

Rather than a ritual, let's think of this as a friend introducing you to a whole group of people you really should know already. Candles and a nice floral oil and incense are still in order. And a good workout with the MOON MAGIC AURA CLEANSING EXERCISE is the best way to complete your preparations. Then, sitting with that lovely shaft of moonlight coming straight to your heart, address Isis: "Loving Mother Isis, I recognize the need to get acquainted and cooperate with my personal band of spirit people. Please join me in your role of Diana, and assist by introducing us, and helping us to establish a better working relationship. I invite you to visit me here at my altar now, and begin the happy introductions.

This is the time to let your imagery bridge the gap and bring you the reality of simple spirit contact. See lovely Diana float down the moonbeam and materialize beside you, not as a solid form but in a shimmering body of LIGHT. If you're used to seeing AURA, you'll notice that Diana's form and texture is just like that of any other AURA, though perhaps a bit brighter. When she is very close to you, you will find it much easier to observe her in your altar mirror than to look directly at her. Also, it is in this way that you can be introduced to your spirit people. You will see filmy shapes of light (usually bright gold, green or violet as their predominant color). They will tend to come into sharper focus one or two at a time as Diana introduces them to you personally. The whole process will vary tremendously from one time to another, or even from one spirit to another at the same sitting. The first few times you try, it may seem too hazy or jumbled up to make sense, but do stick with it—a strong part of the initial get acquainted phase is on the pre-conscious or subliminal level anyway, and it will grow in clarity and detail with just a few weeks of regular practice.

You may not be sure whether it is imagination or you are really seeing the subtle AURAS of your spirit friends, but this is the time to hang in there and bring it fully into your reality dimension—and as you do, you are validating all the work you have done previously while relying on just your image-making faculty. If you have won this battle on the basis of a growing mound of results from your earlier work, the realization of the reality should be pretty easy. But for all of us, the thing I call the front mind (perhaps best called intellect) is certain to resist this threat to its supremacy. This is the time to convince intellect that it is in its best interest, as well as the best interest of the complete organism, to relinquish its pseudo-supremacy in favor of a practical working partnership with the creative pre-conscious and magical sides of your beingness. It may take several sessions to fully establish the reality, but now is the time to do it.

GETTING TO KNOW YOUR SPIRIT FRIENDS AND HELPERS

Since Diana and your spirit people are manifesting themselves to you in their natural auric state rather than the denser forms possible only in special circumstances, it is not reasonable to expect them to speak aloud to you. But, they can think a thought apparently inside your head almost as easily as you can. This is an excellent communication system if you simply accept it as fact and pay attention. If you have already communicated this way with a thoughtform, you understand, and if not, it will better prepare you for that part of our work, too. The important point is to enter into the spirit (pun intended) of the thing. Sense the "spoken" thoughts of Diana and your spirit people as she introduces each one; notice the identifying features in their AURAS and get the feel of their thought processes inside your head. Give enough careful attention and interest to recognize the members of your spirit band as individuals, and let the bonds of friendship begin to grow naturally between you. Remember that friendship has a way of growing naturally out of shared experiences. Your spirit people have been with you through many experiences, but your lack of conscious awareness of it has kept it from being truly shared. Now that you have been formally introduced, it is the ideal time to cultivate your awareness of these interesting people and share the bulk of your daily experience with them as you carry on a running two-way conversation.

TAKE CARE TO CEMENT THE FRIENDSHIP
BEFORE YOU ASK FOR HELP

No one is quite as big a bore as the pest who starts asking you to do favors for him 5 seconds or so after you have been introduced. You instinctively draw back from such a person, and if you must be around him at all, you stay constantly on guard against fresh unwarranted impositions. In the enthusiasm of realizing the potential help available to you, there is a tendency to turn yourself into just that kind of inconsiderate bore to your spirit band. True, this is more nearly a family than a bunch of strangers, but it's best not to let yourself fit the classic definition of a relative: a person you have to be nice to whether you like him or not.

Quite the contrary, this happy get acquainted period is a time to feel the enthusiasm of your spirit friends for your mutual progress and listen to their ideas and suggestions. When you understand the true nature of the relationship, you realize that you should very seldom feel the need to ask for anything. It is exactly the relationship described in the Bible with that wonderful phrase (not a promise, but a simple statement of fact): "Before they call I will answer, and while they are yet speaking I will hear." Pay attention to the chronology in that quote, too; it is of great significance. When the understanding sinks in, you'll find it easy to relax and focus on improving your communications and enjoying the developing spirit friendships.

We should take a minute to talk about the type of people you can expect Diana to introduce as your special spirit band. There can be plenty of variations, especially if you accepted some difficult pre-birth assignments. The number may vary from 3 or 4 all the way to 20 or 30. What we might call the nucleus of the group will be 3 or 4 people you have spent many lifetimes with— sometimes together in physical bodies, but most often taking turns being spirit helpers to the one of your group who is currently inhabiting a physical body. This sets the proper tone of the relationship. These are old friends, associates, and partners in your progress, to be treated as equals with areas of expertise in which their judgment can be respected, but also with their weaknesses or even prejudices to be reckoned with as you do with similar qualities in physically embodied friends. Be especially alert during the introduction period for a distinctive extra tingling sensation when you meet one particular individual. The feeling is that of a mild electrical stimulation that somehow makes you feel hugged all over. This will become a regular greeting from the being I like to call your spirit lover. There is no adequate way to describe the beauty of the deeply intimate and personal relationship the two of you have built over the many lifetimes you have spent together. Here, too, there are wide variations between people. Speaking from the purely personal level, I have to say that my own spirit lover has brought a kind of love, tenderness and absolute support that is far more wonderful to me than any relationship I have enjoyed with a person in a physical body in this lifetime. And all of this has been with a total absence of jealousy or possessiveness of any kind—indeed with plenty of enthusiasm and encouragement for my physical relationships, too!

Continue to invite Diana to help you meet and get nicely acquainted with your spirit band on a regular basis (I'd suggest at least three times a week, or more if you can make the time for it) until you feel that you have established a comfortable working relationship with your spirit people, and they are able to take over the communication process.

THE JOYS AND BENEFITS OF WORKING WITH YOUR SPIRIT PEOPLE

I can't imagine not starting and ending my day by touching base with my spirit people at my altar, and I trust it will develop naturally for you, too. But it should definitely not stop there. The same communication system where you speak aloud (or form your thought as if it were spoken aloud) and the spirit pops the answering (or a new) thought into your head can work 24 hours a day, regardless of where you may be. Your spirit people are not limited by the confines of a physical body, so they can exercise an awareness that almost approaches omniscience. Thus they can see ahead and keep you out of all manner of trouble as well as steer you toward special opportunities for windfalls and achievements of all kinds. Let's share some feedback on this as the best way to show you at least some of the potential.

C.J. explains his working spirit relationship this way: "I am a salesman and my work requires a great deal of driving in and around this big city. Obviously time is money to me, so this is the way my spirit people first convinced me of the great practical value of our relationship. Since I started the communication process, I have never been caught in a traffic tie-up. I get the little thought popped into my head that says, 'Go this way, it will be quicker, So I do and it is. Often I'll hear or read about a big traffic mess that I would have been in if I had not heeded my spirit advice. I've been able to make an average of about one and a half extra sales calls a day that way, and I credit that for about a 20 percent increase in my commission income. But it's much better than that. While talking to a customer, I'm often given suggestions of products to mention, friendly questions to ask that warm up the prospect, and even timing of the close. This has been worth about another 80 percent, so my income has literally doubled as a result of the good relationship with my spirit band. I'd be happy enough with just the income, but there are lots of other good things that are perhaps even better! My family life is much happier, and, best of all, I feel a new meaning and purpose to my life. I'm improving and growing in all areas of life, and my expectations for the future are bright and wonderful. Playing on this team with my spirit people is the most magnificent thing that has ever happened to me.

Bonnie S. sent us this report: "I'm a typical working wife. It's easier now that the children are grown and on their own. But I thought I was entering old age! The doctors diagnosed my problem as arthritis. My fingers were so stiff it was affecting my typing, to the point where I was wondering if I could hang on to my job. The problem came on so slowly, I had pretty well accepted it as an unfortunate part of the aging process. Then I had the marvelous experience of Diana introducing me to my spirit people. It was a fascinating time and I got many obvious manifestations of spirit help. Then, after a few weeks of working with my spirit friends, my fingers were really hurting me as I sat down at my altar. Without really thinking about it, I kind of blurted out, 'Hey, isn't there something that can be done to fix these painful fingers?' And I was quite amazed at the instant response. This was so strong, it was almost as if a loud voice spoke in my head: 'You are allergic to refined sugar, beef and homogenized milk. Substitute other foods, but completely eliminate all forms of these three foods in your diet, and we'll take care of the rest.' It wasn't easy, and I had to do a bit of a selling job on my husband to get his cooperation, but I promised myself to completely honor the spirit direction. And was it worth the effort! In less than a week I could tell that my fingers were more limber, and by the end of the second week I was quite completely pain free. There were lots of little aches and pains I had ignored over the years that disappeared about the same time. I feel 30 years younger! Naturally my marriage is improved, too, since I'm much better company when I feel good. I thank my spirit friends every day, and of course I'm following their directions to make many more improvements in my life.

C.N. reported this way: "Al, I certainly agree with you that my spirit lover is responsible for the most rewarding and fulfilling experiences of my life. I could expound for hours on the beauty of the relationship, but I know that you are mostly interested in reports of practical things, so I'll confine myself to this specific report of help. I own and operate a small business, employing about 10 people. Over the years it has been a very lucrative operation, allowing me to live well and accumulate a comfortable net worth. But, for the last few years my business seemed to quit growing, while inflation kept pushing up my costs. Finally it reached the point where my accountants gave me a report of the last year's operation at a bare break-even point. This meant that I had worked a whole year for nothing! Because my investments were doing well, I was sorely tempted to shut down the business, but I felt a strong loyalty to some of my employees who would undoubtedly have a very hard time finding new jobs. At my altar, I talked the situation over with my spirit people. As I asked for guidance about whether I should close the business, I got what felt like a loving pat on the head from my spirit lover. That was all, but somehow it seemed like enough. And that very night, in the special dream state that you have taught me to call an astral experience, I became aware of my spirit lover perched on top of a big filing cabinet in a very sexy white dress. She seemed to be directing the activities of a group of about 10 other spirits. As I watched, they did the complete engineering of a marvelous new product. This was a Saturday night, and they literally rousted me out of bed at 6 o'clock Sunday morning to bring it into material manifestation. I worked all day getting it all down on paper, and it was what the world calls a 'natural!' The marketing effort was a tremendous success from the beginning, and my business is highly profitable again. I regularly thank my spirit friends on behalf of my employees, who knew nothing about the whole situation, as well as for my family and myself. Al, its wonderful!"

LUNAR SPIRIT CONTACT KINETICS—HOW TO LIVE THE CHARMED LIFE

Without a doubt, you will marvel at the wonderful help you consistently get from your band of spirit friends. It will surely be spectacular enough to interest you in perpetuating the help by using LUNAR KINETICS, but you will find much happy fallout from the practice as well. Since kinetics is always concerned with the dynamics of a situation, the first question we must pose here is: what's in it for your spirit friends? Or perhaps more practically, how do you go about keeping your spirit friends interested?

To some degree your spirit help has been earned in past associations, or assigned as part of a pre-birth agreement. All the same, it's not good to keep drawing out of a bank account without ever putting anything back. But what shall you put back, and how? Certainly the acceptance of the idea of a partnership in evolution with your spirit band is the beginning of practical LUNAR SPIRIT CONTACT KINETICS. Being aware of the special things that your spirit people do for you, and remembering to say thank you, will also add zest and fun to the rapport while it positively encourages them to do more. But it is also essential that you set aside some time at least once a week where you completely forget about your personal pressures, desires and burning interests and pose the question: "Beloved spirit teachers, guides and friends, I know that this is a partnership and I am receiving a great deal of inspiration and help from you. Now, what can I do for you to help balance the scales?" Again, accept the answer in our established way as an idea that is suddenly popped into your head.

Many times your answer will be something like, "Just hold course and speed, and keep working on growth and rapport," but there may occasionally be quite specific requests. Here is another spot for balance and caution. If you ask a question like this when you are working on too low a psychic/spiritual level, you may encounter a joker who will give you one impossible task after another just to enjoy your frustration. I mention this only for balance. In general, you will feel a good rapport with your spirit friends and a real desire to do nice things for them. In turn, a sincere spirit will never ask for something that would be detrimental or make a serious imposition on you. Thus, within the bounds of that very scarce commodity we call common sense, you will enjoy at least an occasional opportunity to partially return the favors to spirit—and there is invariably more happy fallout as a result.

Let's let this feedback from Molly F. help our understanding: "For years I was vaguely aware of spirit presences around me. It was somehow comfortable, but I didn't really understand it until I got into your moon magic work. Then Diana introduced me to ten spirit people who are super special to me, and things have been getting better and better ever since. Without question, I can credit my spirit people with a promotion and big raise, a big improvement in my family life, healing of what had been a chronic back condition, and literally hundreds of little things from parking places to small windfalls of money to uncanny good luck from a super sense of timing. You can be sure that I regularly ask my spirit friends what I can do to help them in return for so much that they do for me. Mostly I just get what feels like a pat on the head and the 'Hang in there, all is going well' thought. But occasionally I get a little assignment, usually to do something to help some other person. For instance, last week I was urged to go to a local bingo game and play one card for me, and another for a family down the street. I won $100 apiece for us, and joyfully headed for the neighbor's house with the money and the explanation that I had a hunch to play a card for them for good luck and it worked. I found out then that the husband had been out of work for several months and they were in bad financial shape, but too proud to ask for welfare. The $100 was a big help to them momentarily, but it was also spirit's way of getting me into the act. I just 'happened' to know of a job opening that was almost perfectly suited to him. For an afternoon of fun I wound up with $100 in cash, a big extra pat on the head from my spirit people, and some wonderful new friends in the neighbors spirit led me to help! Thats what I call happy LUNAR SPIRIT CONTACT KINETICS."

I could give you lots more on this happy subject, but this is another perfect spot to challenge you to get some results of your own—do, and let's have a letter from you telling me about it. I'll give you my mailing address at the end of our final chapter.

MOON MAGIC MOTIVATORS

1. There is a group of dedicated spirit beings striving to work with you for your mutual evolution and good. It is to your distinct advantage to recognize and cooperate with these good people.

2. Use the very informal ritual to invite Diana into your altar room to introduce your spirit friends to you. And remind your intellect that it is to the advantage of the whole organism that it not stand in the way.

3. Don't expect your spirit friends to speak to you aloud. Accept the principle that they can pop a thought into your head—in answer to a question, or to originate a conversation. It will work well with practice.

4. Go gently during the get acquainted period. A little time and experience will show you that you seldom have to ask for favors or help. Your spirit friends are on top of things and see farther ahead than you, so they know what help you need before you do.

5. There may be 3 to 30 people in your personal spirit band or group. As you enjoy getting to know them, be alert to recognize the one you will come to know as your spirit lover. This can be a most rewarding and fulfilling relationship.

6. Keep at the get acquainted process until your communications with your spirit friends are well established, and let the guidance and help prove the value of the relationship again and again.

7. You will want to enjoy the give and take of LUNAR SPIRIT CONTACT KINETICS. The idea of doing nice things for your spirit friends when the opportunity arises is good in itself, and it invariably brings extra good to you in the process. Get your own super results, and write me about them.

Moon Magic
And Pyramid Power

As we continue on the path to fulfillment of your destiny, the next big step involves a more complete mastery of the psychic and subtle energies—that you may better control every aspect of your life expression. The Bible often serves as a good textbook for the creative process. Remember: "In the beginning was the word ... and the word became flesh and dwelt among us." This is another way of saying that each consciously directed physical manifestation begins as a thought—or I prefer to use the energized thought idea in the more accurate term, "thought-form." Thus far in our work we have have learned to work with moon energies and deities in broad terms, quite properly leaving the details to the greater wisdom of the spirits and moon personalities involved in the operation. Now we will work with living thoughtforms and power them with energy from carefully constructed devices to take you another giant step along the path to your complete mastership.

THE NEED FOR PSYCHIC AND MAGICAL "MACHINES"

The second floor of the E.S.P. Laboratory building houses quite an array of psychic and magical devices, some in the experimental stage and others performing various types of serious magical work. Some visitors like to tease me that I'm "gadget happy," but I have a quick way of handling that accusation. I simply ask the visitor how he (or she) got to the Lab. And if he can't say he walked the whole way, I've won with no further discussion. Machines and gadgets are not an end in themselves, but they are the best way that man has yet devised to multiply his effectiveness. In the same time that it takes a normal person to travel 3 or 4 miles on foot, he can go 40 or 50 miles in an automobile, or several hundred miles in a jet plane. Our modern technology and its gadgets permit us to go farther and accomplish more than our grandfathers ever dreamed could be possible, and the same is true of our thoughtforms and magical devices—as we will shortly show you.

We must take care to notice and harness all of the energies that are available to us, and, particularly, we must avoid overlooking the power that is close at hand just because it seems "too simple." One of these close at hand energies is the vibratory power of numbers. Coming down to us from out of the night of time is a square of numbers traditionally tied to the vibratory rate of the moon. Figure 1 presents this "square of the moon." No matter which direction you choose, each column of figures (up, down or across) adds up to a total of 369, the number of the "golden horn" or the moon. Do not cut Figure 1 out of the book; it will not work for you that way. Wait for the first Monday after a new moon, and copy the figure in your own hand on a piece of virgin parchment during the 1st, 8th or 15th hour after sunrise. All the while you are copying the figure, chant: "I bask in the love and protection of my dear Mother Isis." And when you complete the figure, conclude with: "Thank you, Mother Isis, it is finished."

37	78	29	70	21	62	13	54	5
6	38	79	30	71	22	63	14	46
47	7	39	80	31	72	23	55	15
16	48	8	40	81	32	64	24	56
57	17	49	9	41	73	33	65	25
26	58	18	50	1	42	74	34	66
67	27	59	10	51	2	43	75	35
36	68	19	60	11	52	3	44	76
77	28	69	20	61	12	53	4	45

**FIGURE 1: THE SQUARE
OF THE MOON**

You will find it helpful to place the square of the moon on your altar (with the top facing magnetic north) to be used as a good moon energy source. Just touching the figure in place will give you a boost of benevolent energy, and putting a small snapshot of yourself (also with head to the north) in the center of the figure will bring you a steady flow of the same wonderful energy. Let's save our feedback for later and press on to harness more powerful sources of useful energy.

HOW TO BUILD YOUR MYSTIC PYRAMID AND ENHANCE IT WITH MOON POWER

From the Great Pyramid of Kufu at Cheops in Egypt comes our next power source, the energy of shape. While engineers and physicists argue over what it might be, small models of the Great Pyramid demonstrate the power to sharpen razor blades, prevent decay in organic matter and all manner of useful phenomena. In my book, *Miracle of Universal Psychic Power*, I discussed the idea that whatever the technical description may be, this is definitely a benevolent energy with positive healing properties. You may want to review the Pyramid Power chapter in that book for background, but we'll give you enough here to make it work for you whether you feel you understand it or not. Let's work first to build your own model, then we'll turn to practical applications of its power.

Just a touch of elementary high school geometry will suffice for this easy job. You probably remember how to construct an isosceles triangle. A regular piece of writing paper will do for your template. Draw a straight line 9⅛ inches long near the bottom edge of your paper. Then, using a compass or a pencil tied to a piece of string, describe an arc 8⅞ inches from each end of your base line. Where the two arcs intersect is the point of the top of your isosceles triangle. Draw it, then using a light poster board, cut out four of the triangles, taking care to mark the base so you won't be confused. A little scotch tape will put your four triangles together into a 6-inch tall model of the Cheops Pyramid. (If all this sounds too complicated, 6-inch model pyramids are available for sale at a reasonable price from many sources, including E.S.P. Laboratory, 7559 Santa Monica Blvd., Los Angeles, Calif. 90046.)

What happens when we marry the energy of the pyramid shape with the energy of the moon square? It is more nearly a geometric than an arithmetic progression—or shall we say it's clearly a case where one and one add up to considerably more than two! And the marriage can be accomplished by simplicity itself. Just put your fresh new pyramid over your square of the moon, with one face of the pyramid toward magnetic north. If you have your picture on the moon square, you have considerably multiplied the flow of positive energy into your life expression. But this is just the beginning of your new power. Again let's hold off on the feedback while we press ahead to more effective application of the power to making your life happier, healthier, more prosperous, and full of love.

NOT 20-MULE TEAM, BUT 20-MOON POWER MAGIC!

This far we have in effect given you a shiny new car, all gassed up, but awaiting a qualified driver and a place to go. We will quickly qualify you as the driver, and give you the choice of where you want to go—with virtually unlimited range and potential effectiveness. The mechanism is the properly constructed and energized thoughtform. When you do it well, you indeed find yourself working with what we might call 20-moon power! I like to suggest that you begin with short-range goals that you feel are reasonably attainable with a bit of magical help. Get a few quick victories under your belt to get the feel of the complete process before you tackle the really major projects. With this in mind, we're ready to get down to the specifics of how to do it.

Clarity of thought is the keynote here. If you set a fuzzy goal, you're certain to get fuzzy results that will lead you to doubt the effectiveness of the system, so work on writing the goal. Then read it as if you were a complete stranger (or better, a computer) to see if your written statement agrees precisely with what you know you want. The initial power must come from your own positive enthusiasm, so work on your wording to make it as positive as possible and full of the kinds of words that *evoke* your enthusiasm. Let's illustrate with a whimsical example. We'll assume that you are a young girl and want to be invited to a special party, like the senior prom. The initial thought might be expressed, "I want Joe to take me to the prom," but that has two drawbacks. First it limits you to Joe, who may have other ideas about a partner or about going fishing that night. And second, it lacks the punch to generate your enthusiasm. How about reworking it this way, "Let me be taken to have a super good time at the prom by a really wonderful date!" Feel the difference? You can undoubtedly do better by tailoring it more personally, using the words and ideas you know turn you on the best.

When your thoughtform is worded as well as you feel you can do it, we're ready to energize it. On half a sheet of writing paper, draw a neat triangle with its point near the top. Beneath the triangle, write your carefully worded thoughtform request, ending with "Thank you" and your signature. Across the top of the triangle write, "Mother Isis," and fold the sheet in thirds by bringing the top of the triangle down, then the end with your signature up. Slip your picture inside the thoughtform sheet, lay it on your moon square sheet (with your head in the picture to the north), and we are ready to begin the activation process. After a short MOON MAGIC CHAKRA CLEANSING EXERCISE, picture that bright shaft of moonlight coming straight to your heart, see Isis there in the moonbeam and put both hands gently on the thoughtform sheet and moon square sheet. Speak aloud at least three times, "Mother Isis, I joyously accept your powerful help in bringing this positive request into happy manifestation. I thank you that it is so now." Each time you speak these words, pause to picture the end result as you have so enthusiastically written it, and bathe the idea in love and happiness. Then cover your setup with your pyramid, and holding your hands over the whole bit, speak the request and thank you to Isis again, and bathe it all in love again. Once or twice a day, repeat the short rite over the pyramid, and keep your enthusiasm level high until you have the material manifestation in your hands. Then when it is all finished, return to your pyramid and remove the written thoughtform request. Write inside the triangle, "My special thanks to you again, Mother Isis, for helping to bring this wonderful victory." Sign the sheet again, and burn it as you repeat your thanks to Isis.

RESULTS OF 20-MOON POWER PYRAMID MAGIC

I have so much good feedback on this part of the work that it's almost painful to make the decisions on which ones to include here. The few we have room for are quite representative of the kinds of results you should expect. Lets start with this one from D.Y.: "I had been trying to sell my house for just about a year, there were a few prospects, but they seemed not to want to buy it, but to steal it! Finally I realized it was time for the 20-MOON POWER PYRAMID WORK. I worked on my thoughtform and settled on this wording: 'My house is listed for sale at a fair price. Let it sell quickly to a buyer who will both appreciate and enjoy it.' It was easy to work up my positive enthusiasm with that thoughtform wording, and I seemed to feel several comforting pats from Isis as I spoke the request for help over the thoughtform sheet on my moon square. Then in just 3 days, the buyers appeared. They were a sweet couple who fell in love with the house and bought it on the spot without quibbling at all over the price. I left my thoughtform setup intact until the final papers were signed and I had the check in my hands for the proceeds. Then I had a very special thank you session for Isis. It's wonderful!"

G.B. reported this one: "My husband moved out for the third time this year, and it really looked like the old adage about 3 strikes and you're out. But I love him and the children need him and I hated to see 18 years of married life go down the drain. Nothing else I tried had helped at all, but now I'd heard of the 20-MOON POWER PYRAMID bit and decided I had little to lose by trying it. Fortunately we had just passed a new moon, so on Monday I made my square of the moon with happy anticipation. Over the weekend I got my posterboard and had the pyramid already made and waiting. Without waiting for the ink to dry on my moon square, I started the setup using as a thoughtform request, 'Let all negativity be swept away, that P. may realize and accept the love and devotion of his family and return to rebuild the happy life we have shared together.' It was easy to build the enthusiasm for the rite, and as it was finished I felt several suggestions for making the new life happier for P. pop into my head. At another time I might have considered this criticism, but now I took it to heart as my part of the bargain that was to assure the thoughtform's success. A week went by uneventfully. But suddenly I got a phone call from my husband asking if he could come by for a talk. I said, 'Sure,' and he was here in minutes. He told me he had somehow come to look upon the other woman in a new light, and he now felt that his place was definitely with me and his children. He asked my forgiveness, and asked if he could move back in. I told him of the thoughts I had received about making our life happier for him, and tears of joy streamed down his cheeks. We're happier now than at any time in our lives. I thank Isis every day, but I'm leaving that pyramid setup just as it is—I don't want to take any chances."

L.H. gave us this report: "Al, I thought it was just old age (I'm 69 years old) that had me dragging around and wheezing like a dead man, but I finally decided I should go to a doctor. After x-rays and a bunch of stuff, the doctor told me I had an advanced case of emphysema—that if I moved to Arizona at once I might last six months to a year, but if I stayed here in this damp climate I'd be lucky to last three months. And he had no cure to even suggest! Well, all my friends are here as is my home and all the places I like, so I decided there was no future in going off to Arizona to die by myself. In desperation I remembered the moon magic. I felt (quite rightly, I think) that I didn't have time to wait for a Monday after the new moon, so I bought a pyramid and made my moon square on the spot, all the while asking Isis to cover for me about the timing of the thing. The thoughtform was simple enough: 'Let there be complete and perfect healing for me, and vibrant good health.' I got it all set up and working just before bedtime. Next morning it seemed like I spit up a quart of phlegm, but afterwards I seemed to breathe better and I had a little more energy. The process continued for about three weeks—spitting up phlegm in the morning, but every day feeling a little better than the day before. At the end of a month I was feeling wonderful and decided to see what the doctor might say about my condition. He x-rayed me again and had a very puzzled look on his face when he waved the pictures at me and said, 'I don't understand this at all. Today your lungs are in better shape than those of the average 40-year old in good health. I guess you don't have emphysema after all.' I waited another month to tell you, Al, but now I want you to know that I'm healthier and more active than I've been in 20 years. I've just started a new business and I'm planning to marry again soon— she's a cute spring chicken of 52 years! You can bet I thank Isis daily!"

We'll stop with just this one more from D.S.: "That 20-MOON POWER PYRAMID RITE is a real winner! Not long ago I got to thinking of all the nice things I could do with an extra ten thousand dollars, so I decided to try the PYRAMID RITE on it. My thoughtform was: 'Let me find and capitalize on an opportunity for a windfall profit of $10,000 or more.' Believe it or not, the next morning my phone rang with a situation presenting itself. I'll not go into detail, but the buyer of this piece of property that was already lined up needed a name for the offer other than his own. It took all of 15 minutes to do what he needed (all legal, too), and I wound up with a check for $10,950 for my 'trouble!' I've used about the same thoughtform twice more and picked up one check for $13,250 and another for $11,333 all in the space of about three months. Al, this 20-MOON PYRAMID thing is misnamed. You should call it the 20-MOON POWER gold mine!"

BEYOND THE PYRAMID—EXOTIC MOON POWER DEVICES AND RITES FOR SUPER RESULTS

It is not within the scope of this book to go deeply into the devices and techniques that go way beyond even 20-MOON POWER PYRAMID work. So, this section is in the nature of a special challenge to you. I'll give you a few solid clues, then ask you to try your hand and let me hear of your special results. By pooling our experience and knowledge in this manner we'll move ahead faster—and this is your special challenge: Get some really outstanding results, and write me about them in time to be included as feedback in my next book.

Now let's give you the areas in which our E.S.P. Lab research indicates solid promise of much extra power. First, a coil of copper wire with a loop inside the pyramid will suck the energy right out of the pyramid and make it available for amplification by reasonably normal electrical means to be applied by copper plates to any place within the reach of your lead wires. Next, a good magnet with its north-seeking pole facing north inside your pyramid will add a considerable amount of extra power. Then we come to the idea of the energy of certain gemstones (a la Baron Karl Von Reichenbach and Edgar Cayce) which can be pumped into your pyramid energy system, as can the energy of cones and spirals. All of these systems and devices can be hooked together with the help of tuning capacitors, electrical amplifiers, neo-tesla coils and the like to power your well-constructed thoughtforms with literally invincible energy. I would enjoy writing a whole book on this subject, but it would obviously be far too technical to have a wide enough appeal to be commercially feasible. So for those of you who both tinker and think, I will look forward to being your sounding board as well as swapping ideas and results with you. I seriously invite you to write me about this subject. My address will appear near the end of our concluding chapter.

MOON/PYRAMID POWER KINETICS

When you are dealing with the stronger energies of moon/ pyramid power, your lunar kinetics become especially important. Misfires or even backfires are possible if you make too many mistakes with this powerful magic. So let's use this section to make sure that all goes well and victoriously for you. First it is important to carefully select the goal you expect to achieve with your thoughtform. Challenge it in at least these two ways: (1) Is it completely positive, good for you, and will it hurt no one? (2) Is it really worthy of you and the higher moon energies? Be sure that you can answer an unqualified yes to both before you actually launch a moon/pyramid thoughtform project.

We discussed working and reworking your thoughtform request to make it as positive and full of emotional punch as possible, but we need to stress your mood at the time of performing the complete rite and the twice daily maintenance rites. The actual thoughtform you create, as opposed to the nucleus idea you write on your sheet, partakes more of your dominant mood at the time of performing the rite than of the written words. So be sure that you are feeling good, positive, and that your mind is not on something negative like a pain or a pile of bills. When we get reports of less than positive results, it's invariably because the budding magician was thinking about a pile of bills while doing a money-multiplying rite with the result that the bills multiplied instead of the money—or the pain increased instead of the health. Keep your attitude enthusiastic, your attention focused fully on the mental picture of the positive outcome, and don't be distracted by doubts or thoughts of the negative side. Similarly, during the daily maintenance rites, be sure you don't give your baby thoughtform colic or indigestion by feeding it anxiety or tension. The happy, positive approach will win for you and guarantee you no uncomfortable side effects. We're asking for a good degree of discipline and concentration here, but a good moon magician will have no trouble at all in demonstrating it—and victory after victory!

MOON MAGIC MOTIVATORS

1. Any physical manifestation begins as an energized, consciously directed thought. Or in simpler terms, a thoughtform.

2. Man uses machines to multiply his effectiveness and ability to achieve. Similarly, it is useful to harness the primordial energies with psychic machines and devices to multiply our effectiveness as moon magicians.

3. We begin by harnessing the close-at-hand energies, as for instance the energy of numbers. The numbers of the square of the moon provide an energy flow of themselves, and with it an extra tie to the energy of the moon.

4. Make your square of the moon in the ritual manner, and use it either by itself or as an extra power source for your moon pyramid.

5. 20-MOON POWER PYRAMID MAGIC puts it all together, your devices working with your well-constructed thoughtforms to make you an ever bigger winner.

6. Beyond PYRAMID/MOON POWER there are myriads of potentially super powerful devices. I invite you to experiment along the lines suggested, and let's pool our knowledge and results.

7. MOON/PYRAMID POWER KINETICS will prevent misfires or backfires. Pay careful attention to the worthiness of your goal, your emotional condition, mood, and the discipline to wall out any negativity—and you will win consistently!

Moon Magic, Lore,
And Your Past Lives On Earth

Its fun to confound TV or radio interviewers, and the subject of reincarnation has given me many happy opportunities to do just that. I try to get the interviewer to ask, "Al, do you believe that you have lived other lives on earth before this one?" To which I answer, "Yes, quite a few in fact." Then if he only follows up with, "Then you believe in reincarnation," I answer with a forceful, "No," and pause to enjoy the confused expression on his face before I continue, "But I don't believe in breathing, either. Both are natural things that we have to do whether we believe in them or not." All of this is by way of saying that I have nothing to sell you here. If you firmly believe that you have never lived on this earth until you inhabited your present physical body, this chapter is not for you. Just skip along to the next one, but please don't let this detract from the usefulness of the other material we have for you, both before and after this chapter. Now for you believers and those who don't know for sure, but are curious, let's get down to the business at hand.

HAVE YOU LIVED ON EARTH BEFORE, AND SHOULD YOU CARE?

I have pretty much always agreed with George Bernard Shaw's definition of history as an agreed upon set of lies, and it is boring to me except where it seems able to teach us a lesson or help us avoid a serious mistake. Similarly, personal history, past lives included, offered me little fascination until I realized that there are disciplines and knowledge already gained in past lives which we can can retrieve with considerable ease, and thus quickly gain significant increases in effectiveness. Indeed my first serious foray into past life study quickly led to the writing of my *Helping Yourself with White Witchcraft* because it seemed that every life I looked at somehow involved forms of sorcery and very practical practices of ritual magic. I also viewed some tragic mistakes that let the inquisition "get" me in what might otherwise have been quite a highlight past life, and promised myself not to let that happen again.

But what does all this have to do with you personally? I'll bet you plenty that you have many latent talents and presently unused disciplines brought forward from past lives of your own just waiting to be remembered and put to marvelously practical use in the here and now! And it is the purpose of this chapter to give you the tools and impetus to rediscover them and so greatly enrich the rest of your present life and perhaps many lives yet to come. Let me give you a few clues to be thinking about while we make ready to journey safely back into your past to have a look around. Have you noticed that there are some parts of history that seem to hit you with almost a romantic nostalgia, while other times and places more or less leave you cold? That special feeling is a strong clue that you had a life during its particular part of the past. Similarly, back in school you no doubt found some subjects much easier to master than others—probably because you worked with the easy ones in a recent past life so the memories are fresh and easy to regain. The so called child prodigy clearly fits into this category, but whether or not your past skills are that spectacular, you did bring some collection of special aptitudes with you into this present physical body. And it will be to your advantage to have a look to see how much better you can apply or exploit them. But enough of the preliminaries; lets get on with the meat!

PREPARATION TO VIEW YOUR PAST LIVES

A common deficiency in most methods of probing one's past lives is a fuzziness or lack of detail in the critical areas. You seem to see and be able to describe an old sunset with ease, but should you witness a murder or get into a special blueprint room, your pictures all too often become too blurred to be of much use. So we will take a minor side trip here to get the extra help you will need to see clearly in your past lives, regardless of the situation involved.

In our opening chapter we met the energy personalities associated with each of your psychic centers or chakras as part of our MOON MAGIC AURA CLEANSING EXERCISE. Now we will deepen our acquaintance with the one of them who is most concerned with clarity of communication. Of course we mean your brow center personality, Thoth, and we will turn again to the energy of numbers to make our special connection. Just as there is a square of Isis or the moon, so also is there a square of Thoth or Mercury, and it will serve us well as a contact with Thoth's special brand of effectiveness through clarity of thought and understanding. Figure 2 presents the square of Thoth. Again, do not cut the figure out of the book, but make it with your own hand on virgin parchment. The time of making this figure should be the first Wednesday after a new moon during the first, eighth, or fifteenth hour after sunrise. During the whole time you are copying the figure, chant aloud (or silently if you will be more comfortable that way), "Brother Thoth, thank you for this tie to your special clarity of perception and thought." And when it is completed, "Thank you again, Brother Thoth. It is completed."

8	58	59	5	4	62	63	1
49	15	14	52	53	11	10	56
41	23	22	44	45	19	18	48
32	34	35	29	28	38	39	25
40	26	27	37	36	30	31	33
17	47	46	20	21	43	42	24
9	55	54	12	13	51	50	16
64	2	3	61	60	6	7	57

**FIGURE 2: THE SQUARE
OF THOTH**

Note that your square of Thoth has eight columns which add in any direction to 260, the number the ancients associated with the metal, mercury, and so with the planet and with Thoth. Since this square has fewer columns than the square of the moon, it will fit neatly on top without fully covering your moon square, and that's what we need by way of special preparation. On your altar will be your square of the moon, with the square of Thoth on top, and your picture on top of that. When this is completed, you are ready for the ritual work.

THE LUNAR MIRROR TO YOUR PAST
LIVES RITUAL

For many years I have known and taught others how to see faces from their past lives in a properly situated mirror. But it was not until I got deeply into the work with Isis and my own spirit band on this book that I was given the complete ritual about to be presented here. If you have equipped your altar with a mirror and used it to help Diana introduce you to your spirit band as we suggested in Chapter 9, you are well set up for this ritual. Be sure to have two tapered candles, one on either side of your altar mirror. The ritual should be performed at night, with these two candles as the only light in the room. Astral travel or psychic phenomena oil and incense are most helpful, but musk or jasmine will do if your prefer. Do your best to be sure that you won't be interrupted during this one.

When you are ready, light your candles, turn off all the other lights in the room, light your incense, anoint your brow, throat, heart and solar plexus with your perfume oil, and sit at your altar a comfortable viewing distance from the mirror. Have your squares of Isis and Thoth within easy reach of your left hand, so you can touch the clarifying energy at any time, just like adjusting the fine tuning on your TV set. Begin the ritual itself with our traditional MOON MAGIC AURA CLEANSING EXERCISE. Then let your moon settle down until the loving shaft of light is coming to you directly through your altar mirror and speak, "Lovely Mother Isis, I seek your help in viewing significant scenes and events from my past lives now, that I may remember the lessons and bring forward the skills of the past to improve my present and future. Please invite good Thoth to join us and help convert my mirror into a viewing screen of the past. I await your participation in love and joy."

Then take care to relax and fix your gaze intently on the center of your forehead (brow center), letting your eyes close slightly as they will do quite naturally. Soon the mirror will seem to turn black and there will be a void where your image has been. Don't panic, that's the natural way that Isis and Thoth use to clear the screen in preparation for the past life pictures. Soon a new face will appear in the place you are accustomed to seeing your own image. Note the strong "family" resemblance—this is your face from a past life. Study it carefully, and as you watch, the picture will begin to fill in other details of dress, surroundings and the like. Soon your eyes will close completely and the picture will be transferred to what seems to be a TV screen inside your head. It is on this screen that you will see in 3-dimensional vivid color the equivalent of action movies of the life you have touched. Try not to become too emotionally involved in the action because a strong feeling of fear, anger or anxiety will blow your picture and the contact with it, thus causing you to have to start the whole process over after a few deep breaths to calm back down. Naturally this is not a time for note-taking. Just absorb as much detail as possible in the serene state that insures easy recall at note-taking time, which should be immediately after the conclusion of the ritual. If the picture becomes fuzzy, you can fine tune it by touching the Isis, Thoth squares, of course without opening your eyes.

Let the film run as long as you are comfortable and the pictures are clear. When you feel that you have received enough for the session or that no more is coming now, conclude the ritual by speaking, "My loving thanks to you, Isis, Thoth, and all who have helped. I appreciate the experience and will join you again soon for another session, that together we may make this a truly significant and useful life expression. Again my loving thanks to you all." Then snuff your candles and go immediately to write down notes of the experience while it is still really fresh for you.

HOW TO GET THE MOST OUT OF YOUR PAST LIFE VIEWING

For the first few times you try, the ritual may feel a little awkward. You won't be quite sure what to do with your eyes, whether it's proper to ask questions, and all of the usual uncertainties that go with a completely new experience. Just a few sessions of practice should be enough to relax you to where your eyes take care of themselves with no conscious direction from you, and in general most of the initial anxiety has been dissolved. Also, at first it is best to let Isis, Thoth and your own spirit guides pick the lives and scenes that you are to see. They have your interest at heart and will get you used to the process before they bring you anything too startling. But as you progress in this ritual, it is natural to include a request to see a particular life or a special time or part of a particular life at the opening of the ceremony, and expect to see it in all the detail you want. As you get more and more comfortable in the work, you will be able to ask for instant replays or different camera angles to help gain the fullest understanding, and the pictures will cooperate.

If a scene you are viewing gets too bloody or otherwise uncomfortable, just ask to go forward or backward in time to a more comfortable period while you prepare yourself to look at the hard part, or skip it until such time as you feel a compelling reason to have another look. Also, it is quite normal to recognize people you know in this life playing roles in one or more of your past lives. Often, these old relationships unconsciously color your attitudes toward each other in the present life. In the old traditions these are called karmic relationships, but take care that the term doesn't fake you out in some way. However, a careful look at the past life situation will often help you understand present conflicts or especially strong attachments. One more word of caution is in order here. I have known people to meet, sense a past life relationship and rush into a miserable marriage. Even if you meet a long-lost past-life lover, it is important to get to know him (or her) in this life before making any serious commitments—we change during the course of one lifetime, so after several lifetimes, that person your unconscious remembers and loves may be so different that time will prove you can't stand each other—particularly because you have undoubtedly changed, too. But, enough of the caveats and cautionary comments; on to the good part!

YOUR PAST LIVES ARE A GOLD MINE OF POWER AND USEFUL EXPERIENCE

The simplest way to understand the practical value of looking into your past lives seems to be to share some feedback from the positive experiences of others. Let's let S.F.'s report kick it off: "I disappeared in my mirror rather quickly, but the first couple of times I blew the action picture by closing my eyes too soon. Now after some experience, I know what you mean by, 'Let the eyes handle themselves naturally.' Anyway, I got there and somehow I knew I was in an ancient civilization, the one most often called Atlantis. There was a lot of interesting gadgetry, some obviously more advanced than what we have today. One of these was a flying device distinctly resembling today's tradition of the flying saucer. After a time, I saw me getting into one of these strange flying craft and we soon soared off on what was to be a long journey. We were up so high I felt I could see southern Europe on one side of us and North Africa on the other. I was enjoying the flight and the view when suddenly there was a terrific explosion. Next, I had the weird sensation of watching bits and pieces of my physical body dropping slowly into the sea. When the 'film' ended I sat quietly at my altar digesting the experience. Almost immediately, I recognized how this had colored my present life. I have always been one of the world's worst fliers. Every time a plane I'm in hits even a slight bump, I get nauseated and fill several containers with my last few meals— or that's the way it always was until that lesson. Now, before I get on a plane, I remind myself that the Atlantean experience is not in danger of being repeated, so a rough flight is still to be enjoyed, not to so fill my unconscious with fear that it causes the sickness. And it proved to be a complete cure! I have traveled by air quite frequently lately, and I'm most happy to report that I now fly even in turbulent conditions and enjoy it, without the slightest hint of the old nausea. This has convinced me of the practical value of the past life work, so now I'm planning regular sessions to see how much more comfort and effectiveness it will bring me."

L.A. reported this one: "I guess I'm not your fastest student, it took me six or eight sessions of trying before I ever got the pictures to transfer into my head. But that very first one proved to be worth all the effort, and much more! I was looking at a setting in ancient Egypt where I was something of a fickle playboy. Let's just say I had more affairs going on than any ten men are entitled to. And, of course, I also had a wife, whom I recognized as the woman I'm married to in the present life also. Things were obviously pretty miserable for her, but as I watched she found a way to cure the situation. She slipped a very poisonous snake into my bed after I was asleep and prodded it with a stick until it bit me several times. I woke up just long enough to realize what had happened, and that was the end of that life. It was quite a revelation! I was 'into' the occult for years, and met my wife that way. We felt a strong attraction from the past and married largely on the basis of it. Then she started to change. She became super suspicious and possessive, which of course put some ideas into my head along the lines of that past life. It didn't get as far out of hand this time, but it was heading that way when I got this picture of the past life. I'd like to be able to tell you that it solved all our problems immediately, but I guess life just isn't that easy. When I told my wife she had murdered me in a past life, she exploded and refused to discuss the situation at all. So I set about quietly cleaning up my act and striving to use thoughtforms to wash away her old unconscious memories and improve her attitude toward me. Now after a year of work I know we're making progress. In retrospect, we were right on the brink of divorce or another murder when the past life insight appeared. There's no question about the practical value of this ritual to me."

D.J. had this experience: "I have always had a goodly measure of claustrophobia, to the point that I preferred the stairs to the elevator wherever possible. When I did have to get into an elevator I generally broke out in a cold sweat and had a great urge to break down the doors to get out. I controlled it, but only with great difficulty and suffering. Then, in the past life viewing ritual, I saw myself being buried alive. I was awake in that coffin for what seemed like an eternity. What a lousy way to end a life! Anyway, I got right to work explaining to my subconscious that elevators are not coffins, and with modern embalming laws there's no danger of being buried alive that way again. With lots of throat center energy and pleas for help to Isis, Marduk , and my spirit guides, it took just a few short weeks to burn away the old fear thoughtform. Now I always take the elevator, and enjoy it."

And from a highly successful businessman, B.R.: "I had a high level opening in my company—one that requires a great deal of administrative skill. I certainly didn't have that in mind when I did the past life viewing bit. But as I watched, I saw a man I recognized. I was having business dealings with him which clearly required a great deal of expertise on his part. As soon as the session was over, I tried to place the man and realized I had seen him in our drafting department. My immediate thought was, 'What a waste!' The next day I called him into my office and asked him if he had any aspirations toward my open position. He said he had fantasized being in the position, but hadn't thought I'd even consider giving him a chance, so he hadn't applied. Anyway, I gave him a shot at the job and he is rapidly developing into the best executive I've ever had. I'm busy, so I don't get many opportunities for things like your PAST LIFE VIEWING RITUAL, but after these first results you can bet it's high on my list to try again."

LUNAR PAST LIFE KINETICS—HOW TO KEEP IT USEFUL NOW

Interest in exploring one's past lives varies from the very casual to the occasional student who makes detailed charts including dates of birth and death, name, occupation, area of earth, and highlights for each of his lives going back three or four thousand years; then, when it is finished, he starts again to do the same for each member of his present family, and maybe a few close friends as well. I have to admit that my own interest is not that strong. I am pretty well aware of several of my lives, including some in Atlantis, ancient Egypt, Greece, China and Spain. The one I get the biggest kick out of talking about was in 12th century (A.D.) Turkey where I was a harlot—I really had a ball in that life! But, in general, I see the value of the past life work as a problem solving, inspiration gaining technique. And that is what we should think of in terms of LUNAR PAST LIFE KINETICS.

The idea is as simple as it is useful. If things seem flat, like you're not getting anywhere and lack inspiration, or when there's a problem that has not been solved by your normal approaches, plan the time for a good MOON MIRROR PAST LIFE VIEWING RITUAL. Then preface the ritual itself with a talk with your spirit friends, Isis and Thoth. Tell them what you think you need and ask them to show you appropriate scenes from past lives that will show you how you tried to solve similar problems before, or that will give you fresh challenge and inspiration. Then enjoy the ritual, and bring back the help you need. This is also a good reason to perform the ritual at least once every couple of months so you will stay sharp and be able to use the ritual with confidence when you need it. On the personal level, the initial impulse and inspiration of each of my last five books has come from PAST LIFE VIEWING work, as has much of the inspiration for the exotic psychic research we conduct at E.S.P. Lab.

It has worked very well for others, too, as this report will help to show: "I must ask you to keep me completely anonymous, but the help I have received from your LUNAR KINETICS idea of PAST LIFE VIEWING for problem solving must be shared. I will try to explain this with a minimum of hedging and disguising of the situation. In my highly sensitive position, I'm pretty well used to sticky problems with very high stakes, but this one I considered to be of real worldwide import. I had worked out a plan, but perhaps because of the consequences of a mistake I felt quite uneasy about it. Fortunately I thought of the past life thing, so off to my altar I went, late at night. I outlined the problem and my planned solution, and asked if there was past life or historical data that might help me finalize the decision. They almost hit me in the head to get the pictures going, such was the importance my spirit people attached to the operation. And I saw quite a show. There, in Atlantis, I was in a similar position facing a similar problem and tried an almost identical solution—with disastrous results. I was able to get a couple of replays and zoom shots to see what went wrong and how. All of this caused a major change of plan, which seemed to be enthusiastically accepted by my spirit people. Al, the magnitude of the thing is so great that I have no way of telling you how many people were saved from untold suffering, along with preserving and even enhancing my position as a result of the success of the changed plan. At the very least, that hour of ritual work saved my whole career. I dare not comment further on how much more was saved as well. Do share this in this way if you can."

MOON MAGIC MOTIVATORS

1. I have no reason to try to sell you on the idea that you have lived other lives on earth before this one. If the subject does not appeal to you, just skip this chapter, but don't let it detract from your enthusiasm for the rest of our moon magic.

2. The historical part of your past lives may be boring to you, as it is to me, but the value of probing them is in gaining new insights, finding latent talents, discovering the causes and so the ways to get rid of many chronic problems, and in general gathering techniques and data of use to you in the here and now.

3. Prepare your square of Thoth to help in fine-tuning the pictures that will come during the ritual itself.

4. Use the LUNAR MIRROR TO YOUR PAST LIVES RITUAL enough times to get comfortable with it. You will get useful information in the process, and have it for a tool when you may need it in an emergency situation later.

5. The practical value of your PAST LIFE RITUAL work will be enhanced with practice as you learn to get instant replay, multiple camera angles, zooms and the like to help you get all the details you need.

6. LUNAR PAST LIFE KINETICS will help you with problem solving and finding fresh inspiration to get past those flat periods. Use it often enough to keep the technique fresh and available for you when you need it.

Moon Magic
To Handle Bosses, Parents, Children And Other Difficult People

At least occasionally, we all encounter a person who seems to delight in taking the adversary position, and all too often it is somebody we live or work with, and so, at least in the short run, we're "stuck with" them. It's important to your overall effectiveness and well-being to move quickly to resolve these conflicts before the antagonism thoughtforms get too firmly established. Let's get right at the mechanism and the magic.

THE MAGICAL POWER OF YOUR MENTAL IMAGES

The classic positive approach to this kind of problem solving is to begin by asking the question, "What is there in me that brings out this negative quality in the other person?" The first place to look for the answer is your own mental image of the person who has apparently become your adversary. There is a special magic to image—normal people unconsciously pick up your image of them and strive with great diligence to live up (or down) to it in their relations with you. Naturally, when a conflict develops, your image of the person tends to become tarnished; your adversary unconsciously senses the change and adjusts his (or her) attitude and actions toward you. Thus, the conflict is deepened, and it will continue to get worse until one or both of you recognizes the problem and sets out to deliberately improve the situation.

Since you are an intelligent person, there is no need to dwell on this point. Let's say simply that the place to start in resolving any conflict is to clean up your image of the apparent adversary, and strive to treat the person in accordance with that positive image. You will be amazed at how many times this is all it takes to get the relationship back on a positive track. But, for the tougher cases, it may be necessary to use a ritual to get your positive image "written on the moon." Lets begin the preparatory work for that now.

HOW TO PREPARE FOR THE POSITIVE IMAGE WRITTEN ON THE MOON RITUAL

We will need strong ties to two more of the moon magic deities for this ritual. And again, we will turn to the power of numbers for the special contact. Figure 3 gives you the contact with the root chakra deity, Nergal. Again, do not cut out the figure; it is to be prepared ritually on virgin parchment during the 1st, 8th or 15th hour after sunrise on the first Tuesday after a new moon. As you are copying the figure, continuously chant (aloud or silently as conditions seem to direct), "Thank you, Brother

Nergal, for your creative power to put acceptance and attractive-
ness into my AURA and so help to restore harmony to all my
human relations. And when it is finished, "Again my thanks,
friend Nergal, for your help. It is finished."

Note that the square of Nergal has five rows and five
columns of figures. Five is the number of change, so you will also
recognize the relationship of Nergal to the vedantic god, Shiva.
The rows and columns all add up to the number 65 which is the
number of Nergal (or Mars if you prefer), and which, by the
numerological technique of adding the digits $(6+5=11)$, reduces
to the very spiritual power number, 11. Mars is often thought of as
the god of war, and this firmness of power is good for us, but the
use here is almost completely in the enhancement of your animal
magnetism, that all other people may give more importance to
your presence, feelings and opinions.

11	24	7	20	3
4	12	25	8	16
17	5	13	21	9
10	18	1	14	22
23	6	19	2	15

FIGURE 3:
THE SQUARE OF NERGAL

4	14	15	1
9	7	6	12
5	11	10	8
16	2	3	13

FIGURE 4:
THE SQUARE OF MARDUK

Figure 4 presents the square of Marduk. As before, copy this figure on virgin parchment during the 1st, 8th, or 15th hour after sunrise on the first Thursday after a new moon. While copying the figure, chant, "Thank you, mighty Marduk, for your power to break up negativity and return my human relations to the harmonious, creative state." And when you finish the figure, "Again thank you, friend Marduk, it is finished."

Note that there are four rows and columns in Marduk's figure. Four is the number of stability and thus a comfortable harmony. The rows or columns add up to 34, the number of Marduk (or Jupiter if you prefer). And 34 reduces numerologically $(3 + 4 = 7)$ to 7, the number of spirituality.

When the two squares are finished, they can live on your altar on top of the moon and Thoth squares. Note that, placed in the order we have made them, each is smaller than the one before, so it can go into place without obscuring the power of the others. These squares plus your normal altar candles and protection or jasmine oil and incense complete the basic preparations for the ritual.

PERFORMING THE POSITIVE IMAGE
WRITTEN ON THE MOON RITUAL

There is a bit of moon lore generally blamed on Pythagoras that involves seeing your affirmation written on the moon. The idea was to write your message on a big mirror, then hold it in a position such that the full moon's reflection in the mirror gives the illusion that your message is indeed written on the moon. Tradition says it worked for Pythagoras, but on the practical level it has many limitations. In fact, I tried it with several sizes of plain, convex and concave mirrors with, to me, totally unsatisfactory results. So I arranged my own session with Isis and Diana to get clarification and modernization for this ritual, and I give it to you now exactly as it was given to me and tested by the members of our research group—with excellent results.

One final bit of preparation is to write out your positive affirmation as a law of the universe, exactly as it is to be written on the moon. State it as firmly and positively as your command of the language will allow. Let's assume that your name is Jim Smith and your problem is with a boss named Joe Jones; then your affirmation might read: "All antagonism is permanently dissolved. Joe Jones accepts Jim Smith as a valuable human being to be treated with respect and understanding. Perfect communication, cooperation, acceptance and effectiveness is the law of this relationship now and forevermore. So mote it be." I will take care to get you other useful examples of positive affirmations in the feedback on this ritual. Meanwhile, we are ready to start the ritual itself.

Anoint your brow, throat, heart and solar plexus chakras with the perfume oil, light your candles and incense, and open with the MOON MAGIC AURA CLEANSING EXERCISE as usual. With that gorgeous shaft of moonlight coming straight to your heart, speak: "Lovely Mother Isis, I seek your special help in resolving what has been a difficult human relations problem for me. Please join me here at my altar and bring our friends, Thoth, Nergal and Marduk to participate in a ritual to write my positive image on the moon as a law of the universe." See, sense, feel or imagine if necessary, the presence of the four powerful beings right behind you and continue: "Greetings, good friends, let's enjoy this happy and productive time together."

Put your left hand on the set of parchment squares to Isis, Thoth, Nergal and Marduk. Feel the power flowing into your body; then raise your right hand and hold it with the palm facing the image of the moon in front of you, and will the power to flow out of the right hand to make a strong connection with the moon. Hold this energy pumping position and speak: "The circuit is now complete. The power of Isis, Thoth, Nergal and Marduk join in writing as a law of the universe in Nergal's red energy on the moon that: (here you speak aloud the positive affirmation you have prepared)." Repeat it three times, then pause to watch as a great hand moves across your image of the moon writing your affirmation in red. When you see that the writing is complete, speak again: "It is finished, and clearly written on the moon as a law of the universe so it must manifest without delay. My loving thanks to all who have helped. I will sit quietly now to receive any guidance or direction that you may have for me. Again my heartfelt thanks to all. So mote it be."

Then return your hands to a normal, relaxed position and try to reach out with your AURA as if to hug or shake hands with the moon deities who are there with you. Stay relaxed and receptive to the good advice or just the good fellowship that is there for you. When you feel that the session is finished, snuff your candles and go quickly to make written notes of anything you should be sure to remember.

RESULTS OF WRITING YOUR POSITIVE IMAGERY ON THE MOON

E.D. gave us this report: "My daughter, G., got in with a bad crowd and began to give me fits. She showed absolutely no respect for authority, kept weird hours, looked awful all the time, was surly to me at best, and I was deathly afraid that she would get pregnant or into even worse trouble. Trying to talk to her was completely impossible—sometimes I'd swear there was even a language barrier! Anyway, I'm sure you get the picture. Since my husband was killed fighting a fire 5 years ago, I've been the only parent, and there seemed to be nobody and no place to turn to for help. I tried changing my image of her, to see her as the well-mannered, solid citizen I thought I had raised her to be, and there seemed to be a little improvement for about a week. But just when I got my hopes up, she had a relapse and started acting worse than ever. Since she is only 17, I felt completely responsible and still desperately wanted to help her. My last hope seemed to be the POSITIVE IMAGE WRITTEN ON THE MOON bit. And how I worked over the wording of my image!! Finally I settled for: 'G. is a sensitive, positive and responsible child of God. She is neat, considerate and productive, a fun loving but effective citizen. She is expressing her good qualities ever more wonderfully now and in the future.' Compared to that task, the moon deity squares were a cinch, timing and all. The ritual itself was delightful, as have been all of my contacts with the moon personalities, and I felt good as I saw the image written in bright red on the moon. But, best of all, it worked! G. started to respond at once. She told me that she realized what a bad influence some of her friends had been on her and that she was exercising her choice of associates more carefully now. Her grades went back up and she finished high school with honors. She's in a good college now and doing very well. I know I don't have to worry about her any more. She is a successful and happy solid citizen. My thanks to all."

I.S. gave us this interesting report: "Al, you left one out when you said, 'How to handle bosses, parents, children and other difficult people.' My problem was with an arrogant, pushy and completely uncooperative employee. Since we are in civil service and she is part of an ethnic minority, it would be just about impossible to fire her. So my only recourse seemed to be some kind of magic. I started on image and really tried to treat her as a competent, cooperative worker, but she responded by taking even more advantage of the situation. This caused me a degree of doubt about the whole magical process, but after I thought it over, I obviously had nothing to lose by keeping on. So, I began preparations to get my positive image written on the moon—WOW! Did that need to be a law of the universe! I decided that my best shot for the image would be: 'M. is fully recovered from her erroneous habits of anti-social conduct. She is a loyal and dedicated civil servant, eager to give her government full value for the money it pays her. She is learning to be friendly and cooperative with her fellow employees and supervisors, and is striving to earn her promotion.' It seemed like a tall order, but that's what magic is all about, isn't it? Anyhow, it took a while to get all the moon personality numerical squares properly prepared, but the night I ritually finished the last one, I put it all together and had my ceremony to get the POSITIVE IMAGE WRITTEN ON THE MOON as a law of the universe. It looked beautiful in big bright letters on my huge moon, and the change in M. was dramatic. She improved at once and soon came to me for guidance, saying she realized she had been less than a model worker before but now she wanted to reform and learn to earn a promotion. I hated to lose her last week when her promotion came through and caused her to be transferred to another department. But it's clearly a beautiful manifestation of good magic—and most wonderful, it significantly helped us both, as no other course of action could have. Thanks for introducing me to moon magic.

"I was afraid we would have to put my father into a nursing home," reported L.V., "But there were so many drawbacks—I couldn't figure how we could afford the extra expense, and it would be a terrible blow to his morale. But he was so cantankerous and absent-minded, we were deeply concerned about his safety and our sanity. Anyway, as a last hope I decided to try the POSITIVE IMAGE WRITTEN ON THE MOON RITUAL. I worked on my written image of him while waiting for the right time to finish my moon deity squares, and settled on, 'My father is a pleasant, rational gentleman who is enjoying his retirement while finding positive outlets for his interests and energies. He is cooperative and a joy to all who associate with him.' And there has been a 'miraculous' change. He is doing a wonderful job of living up to his image as the law of the universe. Not only is father happier, but my marriage is a lot more comfortable, too."

TROUBLE-SHOOTING THE POSITIVE IMAGE WRITTEN ON THE MOON RITUAL

There will definitely be improvement in your apparent adversary from your efforts to write your positive image on the moon. But there are sometimes very old and deep-seated conflicts that tend to perpetuate themselves by habit. Also, there are instances where you are naturally so different from each other that you can both be quite totally positive and still have so many honest differences that a comfortable close working relationship still feels impossible to you. We have a good moon magic fix, but it is important not to use it too soon. The first step in trouble-shooting is to go back to the basics. Begin by asking again, 'What is there in me that brings out the antagonism and conflict in the other person?' Follow up by working on your image of the person, and re-examine your written image to see if you can rework it to be stronger. Then do a second POSITIVE IMAGE

WRITTEN ON THE MOON RITUAL. Repeat the whole process at least three times, a week or more apart, before you consider using the REMOVAL RITUAL I will give you now.

This is a slight variation of the POSITIVE IMAGE WRITTEN ON THE MOON RITUAL that should be used only if you are willing to accept the turmoil that generally comes with it. The variation is in the written image which we now convert to the invocative: "Let (use the name of your adversary) be completely removed from my life now in the manner which will bring the highest good to all who are concerned or involved. So mote it be." The reason you must be ready to accept some turmoil from this ritual is there is a 50/50 chance that you will be the one to be uprooted and removed. It is also the reason to specify that the method must bring the highest good to all. Otherwise it would be akin to playing "Russian Roulette."

This report from G.J. will help you understand: "Hi, Al. Surprise! I'm writing you from my new home in San Francisco. I see now why you urge so much caution in the trouble-shooting work for the ADVERSARY REMOVAL thing. Now that the dust has settled, I must agree that it did bring the highest good for all, but it was sure a shocker! I did the REMOVE THIS PERSON FROM MY LIFE WRITING ON THE MOON, and things happened quickly indeed. Our boss got a nice promotion, my adversary was promoted to fill the vacancy and I was transferred from Boston to a promotion here in San Francisco. It's not at all what I expected, but now that it's over I do agree that it was wonderful magic. Thanks for the help and guidance, but do stress to your later students that when you say there's a possibility of turmoil, you're certainly not kidding."

LUNAR KINETICS OF POSITIVE INTERPERSONAL RELATIONSHIPS

In all of our lunar kinetics, we naturally study the dynamics of life—the give and take that keeps things in good enough balance to maintain your growth and progress. Now that we have learned to write new laws of the universe on the moon, we must consider ways to maintain the balance by giving of yourself in positive efforts to help mankind. As is often the case in the process of writing a book of magical practices, Spirit uses many strange methods and opportunities to get through to me with special things they want included. This time I was led to watch an old John Wayne movie, *In Harm's Way,* on the "Late Show" on TV. As I turned off my set at about 3:00 a.m. this morning, a loud and clear thought was popped into my sleepy head. It was: "World War II is the last conflict the United States has clearly won. Korea and the Pueblo Incident set us up to accept defeat in Vietnam as part of the growing habit of politics giving away the victories our military could otherwise win. The habit of defeat is becoming too well ingrained in the United States' collective consciousness, and is seeping too deeply into the consciousness of its individual citizens. Your readers need practice in writing positive images on the moon. Use the lunar kinetics section of this chapter to set up the positive currents of emotion that will return your country to its winning habits of thought and action, and so work powerfully to insure a combination of freedom and world peace."

So let me suggest that you plan to practice the POSITIVE IMAGE WRITTEN ON THE MOON RITUAL about once a month both to sharpen your skills for the times when you will need them and to practice the balancing of your life through lunar kinetics. At these times, use the positive image, "Let the individual citizens of the United States, and therefore their government, experience a rebirth of optimism and the con-sciousness of a winner, that this country may reassert its position as an invincible and positive force for good and peace as it so properly should be. So mote it be." Enjoy the ritual and know that it is so. You will uplift your own life and that of your countrymen each time you perform this ritual.

Then, occasionally, you might consider the same ritual to help the moon magic personalities who are helping you by using the positive image: "Under the guidance of the moon magic personalities and Al Manning, E.S.P. Laboratory is an ever growing force for good. Its research and magical projects continue to bring forth progress and positive help for mankind. So mote it be." And in turn, we at E.S.P. Lab will be joyfully working for you. For more information on this, do write me at the address I will give at the end of our closing chapter.

As well as the giving of yourself for the common good that we have been discussing, there should be other positive work on your LUNAR INTERPERSONAL RELATIONS KINETICS. This, too, involves the giving of yourself. Work to condition yourself to give the extra little things—a smile when someone is feeling low, the unexpected bit of praise that you can think to give, a bit of encouragement at the right time, a helping hand when a stranger is in trouble, a compliment where you might have given criticism. We're not suggesting that you become some sort of Pollyanna; nothing is quite so insipid. But, a sensitive and positive being will naturally seek to be a positive influence on the creatures around him. I have often called this the idea of psychic ecology—working to improve our common psychic environment, just as the material ecologists seek to improve our air, water, lakes and the like. To those who already see the psychic atmosphere, there is no question about the need for such effort. And to all of us who strive in that positive direction, at least one of the lives you improve will definitely be your own. Again, the idea of striving to uplift the world by being a positive influence at your every opportunity completes the LUNAR KINETICS OF INTERPERSONAL RELATIONS and helps to provide the balance that is necessary for your continued growth and progress. Fortunately, you will find it enjoyable and fun as well.

MOON MAGIC MOTIVATORS

1. People instinctively sense your mental image of them, and unconsciously strive with great vigor to live up (or down) to it.

2. Improving your image of your adversary is often all that is needed to turn the opponent into a friend.

3. To prepare for the powerful magic of writing your positive image on the moon, ritually copy the squares of Nergal and

Marduk on virgin parchment on the proper day after a new moon.

4. Spend whatever time and effort is necessary to produce a powerful, positive written image. This is what you will write on the moon as a law of the universe.

5. Perform the POSITIVE IMAGE WRITTEN ON THE MOON RITUAL, and enjoy seeing the new law of the universe written on the moon in Nergal's bright red energy.

6. Practice the change of image, and the POSITIVE IMAGE WRITTEN ON THE MOON RITUAL at least three times, one week apart, before you consider the trouble-shooting ritual.

7. When you are sure, and are prepared to handle any resulting turmoil, use the "REMOVE THIS PERSON FROM MY LIFE" invocative in the WRITTEN ON THE MOON RITUAL, and win.

8. Both the working for upliftment of mankind and the extra giving of yourself on the personal level are parts of effective LUNAR INTERPERSONAL RELATIONS KINETICS. Practice these faithfully to maintain the balance necessary to your continued growth and progress.

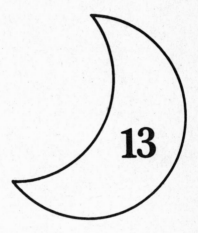

13

Moon Magic
For Success In Gambling
Or Finding Hidden Treasures

Everybody likes to win, and I'm sure that you are no exception. Indeed, building the consciousness of a winner is a major part of becoming a successful moon magician, so a little excursion into games of chance and treasure hunting is quite a proper part of our study of moon magic. It is important to recognize that, in almost every form of gambling, you find yourself in one way or another up against "the pros," so it will take a combination of intelligence, good magic and help from the moon deities to become a consistent winner.

THE WINNING TRIANGLE—YOU, YOUR
HIGH PRIEST OR PRIESTESS AND THE
MOON AS DIANA

The sophisticated magic that is necessary for major windfalls and gambling wins must take place with perfect coordination on three levels—your personal magic, the magic of your spirit band as represented by your high priest or priestess (whom I prefer to call your spirit lover), and the help of the universal moon magic personalities as represented by Diana. Your part is the setting of the proper mood, the clarity of your imagery and incantation, and the performance that keeps it all fun for the spirits and moon magic personalities working with you. Note that I made no mention of need or even worthiness for this type of magic. Clearly, neither of these have any bearing on the element that people generally call "good luck." No! "Good luck" is a product of good magic, though in many cases the magic may have been on the unconscious levels of the winner.

The second level, as coordinator and mediator between you and the power from the higher beings, is equally essential to your magical success. This requires a very close personal relationship with one special member of your spirit band. Indeed, it requires a very real love affair with the one I like to call your spirit lover, but who naturally also doubles as your high priest or priestess. If you have not yet developed that deep a relationship, it is best that you go back to the work of Chapter 9. Take all the time it takes to do this part right; it will bring you many wonderful side effects as it prepares you to become an ever bigger winner.

The lunar kinetics from our last chapter will help you establish a good working relationship with the moon personalities on the basis of your honest effort to help and uplift mankind. But we need to bring in one more, the lovely lady and teacher we know as Bast, your crown center moon personality. Bast is of course another name for the influences we associate with the planet, Saturn. All too often the astrological types will tell you that Saturn is a malefic, or at least a hard and mean task master—but that aspect of Bast is experienced only by those who have neglected to develop a few of the basic disciplines. Bast is the lovely spiritual being who takes great care to see that the world brings you exactly what you deserve, and since you know now that you deserve only the best of everything, Saturn (or Bast) is obviously your best friend as well as benevolent teacher. We will use the magic of numbers once more to produce the proper vibrational tie to Bast. Figure 5 presents the square of Bast. Again, do not cut it out, but plan to copy it ritually on virgin parchment. The process should be performed on the first Saturday after a new moon, during the 1st, 8th or 15th hour after sunrise. While you are copying the square, keep chanting: "Wonderful Bast, thank you for this strong connection to your spiritual power and disciplined effectiveness." And as you finish, "Thank you again, good friend Bast, it is finished."

4	9	2
3	5	7
8	1	6

FIGURE 5
THE SQUARE OF BAST

This is where the research stopped, and I was ready to go on into the ritual work. But there came a tap on my shoulder and the question, "Would you really leave your special friend, Ishtar, out of a ritual like this?" So we have the happy extra of adding power to the moon lore traditions by including Ishtar. Figure 6 presents the square of Ishtar (often also called the square of Venus). Copy this one as with the others during the 1st, 8th or 15th hour after sunrise on the first Friday after a new moon. During the copying process keep chanting, "Thank you, Brother Ishtar (or Sister if it feels more comfortable to you), for this special contact with your wonderful energy of effectiveness." And when you complete the figure, "Thanks again, Brother Ishtar, it is finished."

You should now have 6 magic squares ranging in size from the largest (moon) to the smallest (Bast). These should be set up on your altar in order of size with the moon square on the bottom, then Thoth, Ishtar, Nergal, Marduk and Bast in that order, with Bast on top and of course the tops of the figures facing north. Be sure that your set of squares is within easy reach of your left hand so you can touch it during the ritual. Complete preparations for the winning triangle ritual by gathering lucky, prosperity or frankincense oil and incense, seeing that you have green, white or blue tapered candles on your altar, and fixing a bit of your favorite party food and drink to symbolically share with your friends during the ritual.

22	47	16	41	10	35	4
5	23	48	17	42	11	29
30	6	24	49	18	36	12
13	31	7	25	43	19	37
38	14	32	1	26	44	20
21	39	8	33	2	27	45
46	15	40	9	34	3	28

FIGURE 6:
THE SQUARE OF ISHTAR

HOW TO PERFORM THE WINNING TRIANGLE CELEBRATION RITUAL FOR WINDFALLS AND SUCCESS AT GAMES OF CHANCE

Light your candles and incense, anoint your brow, throat, heart and solar plexus centers with the oil, and open with the MOON MAGIC AURA CLEANSING EXERCISE as always. Still basking in the shaft of moonlight to your heart, place your left hand on the magic squares and speak to Isis: "Mother Isis, I invite you to join me in your role of Diana that we may enjoy the WINNING TRIANGLE RITUAL CELEBRATION together. Please take your place as the representative of the moon deities at the right point of the triangle behind me." See or sense the bright astral form of Diana float into position about two feet behind you and a foot to your right, and greet her: "Beautiful Diana, thank you for the joy of your presence and the privilege of working with you."

Next, address your high priest(ess)/spirit lover by name: "(Lover's name), please take your place at the left point of our triangle that it may be complete and the ritual fun may begin." See your spirit lover's nice AURA float into place, thank the spirit as you did Diana, and you are ready to start the celebration ritual.

Lift your glass in salute to Diana's AURA as you see it in your altar mirror, and speak: "I toast you, Diana and all the moon deities you are here to represent. In the spirit of fun and good fellowship, let the party begin. Then drink, and salute Diana with your glass again. Now lift your glass in salute to your spirit lover as you see that AURA in your mirror, and speak: "(Lover's name), I toast you and all the members of my spirit band you are here to represent. I enjoy this opportunity to socialize with you." Drink, and salute your spirit lover with the glass again. Set your glass down, pick up a bit of the food and salute both Diana and your spirit lover with it, and speak: "Now I symbolically share food with you that we may feel the comradeship of eating and drinking together," and eat in the company of these good friends.

When your mouth is clear again, talk with your friends: "Good friends, I recognize that part of building the consciousness of a winner is an effective, working triangle including all of you. I am worthy of your cooperation because I am sincerely striving to live the magical life, and my success will contribute to the uplifting of the consciousness of the whole species. But worthiness is not really in point here. It is fun to win, and even more fun to play on a winning team. And we are a winning team! We are the perfect winning triangle, now and forever. This party is to celebrate our happy association and the fun of the many victories to come. I promise to stay constantly alert to your guidance to the opportunities to win at games of chance and to be in the right situation to pick up the happy windfalls that will bring the good things of the material life along with our joy of winning. I will sit quietly for a few moments now to see if you have specific suggestions for me, and I will stay alert to your promptings always. Thank you for the joy of playing the game of life on this winning team. So mote it be."

Don't fret if you goof up the words a bit, it is the spirit and true meaning that is important here, not precision in speaking like a parrot. Indeed, a parrot will get no response, but a happy human being exuding the spirit of fun will be propelled from victory to ever more glorious victory. If nothing seems to come at this quiet time, know that your friends will get through to you at any time they want to point out an opportunity. When you feel that the session is finished, toast your friends once more, thank them for the joy of the association, snuff your candles, and go to make notes on any suggestions that may have come through.

RESULTS FROM THE WINNING TRIANGLE CELEBRATION RITUAL

A quick response on the tangible level is often generated by this ritual. M.D. sent us this happy report: "I was nearly destitute when I tried the WINNING TRIANGLE CELEBRATION, but it was great fun to enter into the spirit of the ritual. And the result was even nicer. During the quiet period, I didn't see or hear anything, but I got a strong feeling about a number. So I played it the next morning and won $1,600! My joy knows no bounds! If I ever doubted the reality of the unseen side of life, I don't anymore. My spirit friends and moon deity friends are truly magnificent!"

S.H. reported this experience: "I was invited on a trip to Las Vegas for a couple of days of play. This seemed like a good time to try out the WINNING TRIANGLE thing, so I did it, mostly for a lark. But I did take along a blank keno sheet saved from a previous trip. I didn't quite know why, but it seemed like the thing to do. Just before the period of silence I added, 'You know I'm about to go to Las Vegas, any suggestions?' In the silence that followed, I got the urge to pick up the keno sheet and noticed that some of the numbers on it seemed much brighter than the others. I marked them on my sheet and had the feeling that I should stick with them for every time I played keno on the trip. On that short trip I won first $12, then $144, $12 again and a little later $1,600, all at keno! That, plus 6 nice jackpots on the slot machines, and I came home with something over $2,000 more than I left with. Al, I honestly never had a winning trip like that before in my whole life. This is wonderful, and I begin to understand what it means to have the consciousness of a winner!

"My poker group is threatening not to let me play anymore," reported G.W. "I'd been playing with these people for over 3 years and generally came home a little in the hole. I didn't lose much, but it had been consistent. Then I tried the WINNING TRIANGLE RITUAL before going to the game. And, believe it or not, I came home the biggest winner of the evening! So I did it again before the next game and won big again! Now that I've been the big winner for 8 weeks in a row, they're all teasing me that I spent 3 years setting them up for the kill, and maybe they shouldn't let me in anymore! It really is fun to be a winner, and the rapport with spirit from this has carried over into all areas of my life. I'm doing better on the job, my home life is much improved, and I have the happy feeling of real spiritual growth coming out of the special relationship with my spirit and moon personality friends.

HOW TO PICK WINNERS AT THE HORSERACES

Different people are interested in different games, and so it is with your spirit people. You can be sure that few, if any, members of your spirit band are experts at picking the ponies, but it only takes one. And if you don't have one, your spirit band can help attract or invite one to play with you. We had our clue from S.H.'s report on preparing to play keno. Take a racing form to your altar area and enjoy a WINNING TRIANGLE CELEBRATION RITUAL with your friends. Then, just before the pause to be silent, say: "Good friends, I'm planning a little trip to the race track tomorrow. Do we have an expert who would like to pick me a few winners?" Then relax and see how it comes. You may see the name of a horse seem to stand out as if it were in bold print on your form; there could be the urge to read the horses' names aloud and mark the one that your friends seem to respond to; or your spirit people may suggest a way that is all their own. The trick is to keep it in the game spirit, and never push or get uptight. Take what comes on its own terms, and play for fun. Particularly during the get acquainted period, it is important not to bet large sums that would be a hardship to lose. Play, and enjoy learning to be an ever bigger winner!

Max S. reported on his racing activities this way: "I have a hard 8 to 5 job five days a week, so I really enjoy some relaxation and fun on the weekends. The idea of help on the horseraces appealed to me quite a lot, so I tried the WINNING TRIANGLE RITUAL one Friday evening. I was kind of tired, so I didn't get much in the way of response, but I did get three seemingly clear predictions for the next day. And sure enough, I won a nice daily double by virtue of the predictions. In fact, all three of their picks won—definitely enough to get my attention. The relationship with my spirit people has improved steadily, and they seem to enjoy the winning just as much as I do. We're at the point now where I consistently make more money playing at the track on Saturday than I do all week on my job. I thought about quitting the job, but when I talked it over at my altar I got a very strong feeling that the race thing would then look like work to my people, so they wouldn't participate. We'll be talking over looking for a more rewarding line of work soon. Meanwhile, I'm sure enjoying my Saturdays, and the savings account is big enough to handle a good down payment on a nice new house."

HOW TO FIND HIDDEN TREASURES, LOST ARTICLES OR MISSING PEOPLE

It is natural to lump lost articles with hidden treasure in our work because the best way to find a missing article is to treat it as a treasure hunt. Of course, the main ingredient of a treasure hunt is the treasure map, so we must set about making or acquiring one. The logical approach is to use a map with a scale such that you are almost certain that the object of the hunt does exist within its boundaries, but the greater the area covered by your map, the more sittings it will take to pinpoint your goal. Almost any area you choose probably has a commercially prepared map available, but it is also quite reasonable to draw one yourself on a best effort basis. Let's take your map right to the altar and have a go at the process. Begin with the WINNING TRIANGLE CELEBRA-TION RITUAL, and just before the period of silence say: "Good friends, I have here a map that I think should lead us to (here name the object or treasure you seek). Let's turn it into a happy treasure map together. I will be attentive and seek to let you show me its location."

Then, gaze at your map to see if an area lights up or stands out for you in some other way. An alternative method is to pass your hand slowly over the map about a quarter of an inch above it to see if you feel a sensation of heat over one part. If you get enough data to pinpoint your object, just go get it and thank your friends. But many times it will be necessary to draw a fresh map of a smaller area and keep narrowing down the location until it is definite enough to warrant the digging or whatever else may be necessary to physically recover the treasure. You may work with several maps at a time, or vary it in any way that appeals to you just as long as you keep the interest and fun levels high.

If you are a serious treasure hunter and the problem of permission to search other peoples property, etc. is involved, prudence would suggest that you first play treasure hunt as a game with your spirit people, successfully locating articles someone else has hidden around the house to build your confidence level high enough so that it makes sense to involve other people. Also, take care that you don't try to steal something from property you don't own. Take the legal and ethical way, even if it costs you half the treasure. This is the only way to keep it fun and not embarrassing for your spirit people, and so keep them interested in playing the game with you. And, if you have built your confidence level and rapport with your spirit friends by practice, you should find that this technique can also be used to locate missing persons.

I have many good reports of success in using this method to find objects, treasures and people, but this is a good place to simply challenge you to earn yourself a good report for me, and well save the space to have a good look at the lunar kinetics of being a winner.

LUNAR KINETICS OF BEING A WINNER

One of my favorite psychologist/philosophers, Professor Abraham Maslow, loved to define personal growth as *increase in one's ambiguity tolerance*. In my less pedagogical way, I like to call it *raising your price*—but I do mean raising the price of your anxiety. We're all human and still have some lurking fear and anxiety patterns, but it is quite true that one good measure of your spiritual/psychological growth is that it takes more to trigger your anxiety now than it did the last time you seriously thought about it. The gaming instinct is a good way to exercise and measure that kind of growth, and part of your lunar kinetics of being a winner is to produce the personal growth that does indeed raise the price of your anxiety. In a higher sense, that is the reason for stressing the fun and games aspect, both of your relationship with your spirit and moon personality beings and your participation in games of chance. Raising the overall price of your anxiety is one of the best things you can do for your physical and psychological health as well as for the improvement of your relationships with spirit and your spiritual growth.

So, play often, and win more and more regularly as part of your programmed steps to true spiritual growth. Another often overlooked truth is that real spiritual growth naturally brings a fallout of increasing opulence, comfort and health in the more mundane levels of your life expression. So, again our watchword is "enjoy." But what of the fruits of your many winning joint efforts with spirit? Are they yours to enjoy and use as you see fit? Basically the answer is yes, but we mention it as a serious part of lunar kinetics because there are real needs for extra consideration for your spirit people that do arise out of their helping you to win. Naturally, beings who at present have no physical bodies also have no need for the claim on physical goods and services that we call money. But, they may well have a few pet causes or even people in bodies that money can help. Thus we see that lunar kinetics in gambling would include a ready willingness to spend or give of your winnings to further the causes or just help the people that your spirit friends feel an interest in. Always after a significant win, you should hold an extra WINNING TRIANGLE CELEBRATION RITUAL, especially to thank the spirit beings who helped and to inquire if there is something they would like you to do with part of the money. And when you get a suggestion, do give of the winnings freely—think in terms of fertilizing the crops by happy giving under the suggestion of your spirit people. Also, there may be times when the giving is not to be of money, but of yourself in time and interest in the person or cause dear to the heart of your participating spirit people. Then, too, give freely and willingly.

Let's conclude this section with the idea that becoming a habitual winner is much more important than winning one big one. Play for the fun of winning, enjoy the fruits and be willing to share them under spirit direction, and let the consciousness of a winner grow up so completely in your beingness that you know you will be a winner forevermore.

MOON MAGIC MOTIVATORS

1. Building the consciousness of a winner is an important part of becoming a successful moon magician. Enjoy it!

2. Magic that wins at gambling is a blend of yours, your spirit band's, and the help of the moon magic personalities.

3. Make your magic squares of Bast and Ishtar to complete your set of 6 magic squares in preparation for the winning ritual work.

4. Do whatever is necessary to perfect the relationship with your spirit lover/high priest(ess) for effectiveness in the ritual work for successful gambling.

5. The WINNING TRIANGLE CELEBRATION RITUAL will set the stage to make you a consistent winner. Enjoy it yourself and take care to keep it fun for your spirit people and the moon deities, and your success is assured.

6. You can vary the WINNING TRIANGLE CELEBRATION RITUAL to get winning numbers or horses or help in the games of your special interest.

7. By using maps, you can learn to find lost articles, hidden treasure or missing persons as another variation of the WINNING TRIANGLE CELEBRATION RITUAL.

8. Maintain the lunar kinetic balance by your own spiritual growth and your willingness to share or spend part of your winnings on people or projects of special interest to your spirit helpers.

14

Moon Magic
For Miracles—
Lose Weight, Buy A House,
Win The Lottery—Anything!

Moon magic has as many special applications as you can dream up problems. If you have only scanned this book as if it were a novel, there is no way for you to fully appreciate the potential, but for you who have started to put it into practice, the help that is available to you is already becoming obvious. There are ways to apply moon magic to any problem you may encounter. It is our purpose in this chapter to show you how to handle a few more common problems, with the idea that you will then be able to expand your expertise to tailor an effective moon magic remedy for anything you may need.

THE MOTHER ISIS FIX MY FIGURE RITUAL

At one time or another in almost everyone's life we look into a full-length mirror and realize that we're not at all satisfied with what we see. Neglect, stress, poor eating and exercise habits, force of circumstance, or some combination of these and other causes sneaks up on you, and suddenly there you are, 30 or 40 pounds (or more) above or below the ideal weight for your size and bone structure. Or, some of you ladies may feel that nature skimped too much on your bosoms or derrière, and you men may want more of the classic Mr. America look. Nothing is impossible to you as a good moon magician. Let's prepare for the simple ritual that will help you bring about the changes we have been discussing.

Your set of six squares of the moon deities, a pyramid like the one you made for the work of Chapter 10, and a recent picture of you which includes all the areas you want reshaped, should be readied, along with your favorite floral oil and incense and the usual altar candles. Unless there is room to leave this pyramid permanently on your altar, you will also need to cut about a 10-inch square piece of cardboard to use as a base so you can pick up the pyramid setup at the end of the ritual and move it to a nearby place where it can stay without being disturbed. The final bit of preparation is to get two marking pens, one blue and one red.

When all is ready, light your candles and incense, anoint your brow, throat, heart and solar plexus chakras with the perfume oil, and begin with the MOON MAGIC AURA CLEANS- ING EXERCISE. With the bright moonbeam still coming to your heart, speak: "Mother Isis, I need your help in adding beauty to the world by improving the appearance of my body. Please join me now that together we may bring about the changes I so naturally desire." Then see Isis float down your moonbeam and when her AURA is beside you, mentally invite your spirit lover to the other side. Pick up your picture and speak: "On this picture we will draw the body's features as they are to quickly be. We will color the parts to be reduced in size with blue, and the parts to be enhanced in size with red." Then, use your marking pens to direct the energies to the total reshaping process (or if this is a repeat of the ritual, color the same areas again). It is better to exaggerate a little than to be skimpy with your colors, so delight in indicating a caricature of the ideally shaped you on the picture. When you are finished with the pens, put them down, hold the picture up for Isis and your spirit lover to see, and speak: "Good friends, I know that you join me now in loving the beautiful shape we have outlined for my body. Our love activates the powerful thoughtform, and the energy of the six magic squares will sustain and power it to a wonderfully successful conclusion."

Lay your picture gently upon the six moon deity magic squares with your head to the north, and speak: "The magic connection is complete. My metabolism, appetites and activities are hereby adjusted to bring about these beautiful changes in the fastest manner consistent with maintaining my excellent health. I will cooperate fully with the guidance of my spirit helpers and moon personality friends in the furtherance of this goal. My loving thanks to all who are helping." Cover the picture and magic squares with your pyramid, and if you have a different permanent place for the setup, move it now. When you are comfortably back at your altar, speak: "Mother Isis and all the good friends who are helping, my special thanks to you again. I will strive to stay alert for your guidance and to cooperate to the fullest in this happy venture. I will sit quietly now to see if you have suggestions at this time." Then be as relaxed and attentive as possible. When you feel that the session is finished, thank your friends again, snuff your candles and go to make notes on any suggestions you may have received.

RESULTS FROM THE MOTHER ISIS FIX MY FIGURE RITUAL

Y.D. sent us this report: "During the ISIS FIX MY FIGURE RITUAL I got several strong suggestions about diet and exercise. They sounded hard, but as I tried I felt all kinds of enthusiasm and encouragement from the spirit beings around me, and the whole thing became kind of a joint enterprise in good health and beauty. I know you always want to get to the bottom line, so I'll give you the statistics: In less than 6 months of enjoying the new routine and spirit encouragement I went from 34(A),30,39 to 36(C),26,36 and a very happy husband! Thanks, Al for the introduction, and thanks to all who helped. I do love my new figure!"

C.T. reported: "I had rather serious malnutrition as a child and was always small for my age. All through grade school and junior high, the other boys treated me like a weakling and more or less pushed me around unmercifully. Then I found your MOTHER ISIS FIX MY FIGURE RITUAL, thought it interesting, and tried it. While I was still there at my altar, I got the suggestion of a breathing exercise and a short exercise regimen to do twice daily, and I promised to devote the whole summer to body building. Al, before this, my friends had pretty accurately described my chest as looking like a sheet stretched tightly over a bird cage, but all of that is behind me! During the summer, my chest measurement went from 35 to 41 with pectorals that really show. My biceps and triceps look good now, along with a lot of other muscles I never bothered to learn the names of. I'm in high school now and accepted by my classmates as a real human being. I always had a pretty good head, but now with a nice body to carry it around I'm starting to enjoy life for the very first time. More power to Isis and friends, forever!"

DIANA'S LEAD ME TO MY NEW HOME OR JOB RITUAL

Is it time to find a new home or a better job? Maybe you don't need either one right now, but it's a good idea to remember where you saw this so you can find it when you do. Since these problems are akin to the hunt, this is a perfect spot to invite Diana to help, and with Ishtar pitching in too, things should go without the slightest hitch. Preparation includes seeing that your six moon deity magic squares are on your altar along with frankincense or your favorite floral oil and incense. When you are ready, light your candles and incense, and anoint your brow, throat, heart and solar plexus with the perfume oil. Begin with the MOON MAGIC AURA CLEANSING EXERCISE, and with the beautiful moonbeam shining straight to your heart, speak: "Precious Mother Isis, I seek help in the hunt for my new job (or home). Please join me in your role of Diana, and invite Ishtar to be with us now." Enjoy watching Diana and Ishtar float down your moonbeam and see their AURAS take places behind you in your mirror. Mentally invite your spirit lover to take his (or her) place also, and now see the three bright AURAS behind you. Put your left hand on the magic squares, and speak again: "Good friends, I invite you to join in the hunt. I'm seeking the right new job (or house), and I know that by myself it's a nearly impossible task. But with you joining in the happy hunt we can win quickly and wonderfully. I put myself completely under your special guidance and will do my best to follow your directions to our quick victory. I will sit quietly now to see what immediate directions you may have for me, and I know that now or very soon you will lead me to the right place. Thank you all, and so mote it be."

It's important to stay relaxed and not push in the silence. Remember that the theme is the fun of the hunt, so enjoy. Think of it as momentarily holding the sack on a snipe hunt, and if that bit of nonsense doesn't loosen things up for you, don't worry about it at all. If nothing comes, thank your friends for the knowledge that they will get through to you soon. Or, if you got the guidance, thank them for it and right after snuffing your candles, go to make any necessary notes. It generally takes no more than three days to get your results, so if nothing has happened, it is reasonable to repeat the ritual every 4 days until you have won. Let's hear that it worked the first time for you just as it has for so many.

RESULTS OF THE DIANA LEAD ME TO MY NEW JOB (OR HOME) RITUAL

"I was a bit bugged that nothing happened the night of my DIANA LEAD ME TO MY NEW HOME RITUAL," reported D.K., "But I knew it was important to keep up the game spirit, so I joked about it with my spirit lover, and got a pat on the head in return. That night, believe it or not, I had a dream of a lovely place in an ideal location. The dream showed enough details of street signs so that I was able to find it the next day with very little trouble. And I got there just as the "For Sale" sign was about to be put up. The negotiation was concluded on the spot and I have my ideal new home. Please note the change of address with this, and thanks for suggesting the ritual."

S.L. sent this report: "My unemployment insurance payments had run out several weeks ago and things were getting pretty rough for me, but I was so tired of getting rejections that I almost hated to go downtown. It was definitely desperation that led me to try the DIANA LEAD ME TO MY NEW JOB RITUAL, but even with all my panic I was skeptical enough that I could more or less play at it. I was almost like a young child playing a pretend game, but I have to admit that some of the pretend got pretty real—I did see the three bright AURAS with me, and I got a big goose-pimpley hug from my spirit lover as the ritual was finished. But no instruction or direction came, so I went on to bed. I woke up next morning very early, and very eager to go downtown. It was almost as if I were possessed; I was moving swiftly and purposefully, but I had no real idea what I was doing. In this state, I arrived at a building, took the elevator to the 4th floor, walked right into an office and told the receptionist I was there about the job. She looked at me kind of funny and asked, 'You mean the one I'm supposed to call in the ad for but haven't yet?' Without hesitation my voice replied, 'Yes, don't bother to call it in, I'm here.' It really is the just right job for me—I love the people and the work, it pays much more than I've ever made before, the future and growth potential are bright; in short, its wonderful! To say the least I am now a devoted student of moon magic. Thanks, Al and my spirit friends."

THE ARTEMIS/ISHTAR SMOOTH MY MOVE RITUAL

Success in the ritual work to find a new house or job naturally leads to the mess and trauma of moving—and trauma it would surely be without the powerful help available to you from the ARTEMIS/ISHTAR SMOOTH MY MOVE RITUAL. Just as soon as you know where and about when you need to move, get the kind of spirit help that will turn your potential panic into pleasure and efficiency by using this ritual. Musk, myrrh or your favorite floral incense and oil should be readied, along with a small piece of virgin parchment on which you have written in dove's blood ink, "My good friends, Artemis and Ishtar, direct and smooth my move, that I may joyously and effectively slip into my happy new situation. My loving thanks. So mote it be."

Light your candles and incense, anoint your brow, throat, heart and solar plexus centers with your perfume oil, and begin with the MOON MAGIC AURA CLEANSING EXERCISE. In that lovely shaft of moonlight, speak: "Dear Mother Isis, I invite your help in smoothing my upcoming move. Please join me in your role of Artemis now, and invite Ishtar to join us also." Again, enjoy watching your friends float down your moonbeam to take their places as bright AURAS behind you, and mentally invite your spirit lover to slip into place also. When you see the three bright AURAS behind you, speak again: "Thank you for coming, good friends. I ask your special help in making my upcoming move smooth, pleasant and efficient. I have prepared a piece of parchment as an amulet to assist in keeping us in good contact. I ask you to assist in perfecting our contact for this special help as I place my hand on the magic squares and read the parchment now: 'My good friends, Artemis and Ishtar, direct and smooth my move, that I may joyously and effectively slip into my happy new situation. My loving thanks. So mote it be.' (Read the parchment three times.) I know that our contact is established and my help is assured. I will sit quietly now to see if you have any immediate guidance or direction for me. My loving thanks to you all. So mote it be."

Do sit quietly until you feel it is finished. Then snuff your candles, thank your friends again, and go to make any necessary notes.

Let's share just one typical report on this ritual. From Linda S: "My husband's career has involved several transfers, which means moving from city to city. We get help from the company as far as the financial part is concerned, but all of the planning and arrangements fall on me. You'd think I'd get better with practice, but it seemed to go the other way. I was still having an occasional nightmare about the utter chaos and six months of looking for things after the last move when my husband came home with a big smile and a bottle of champagne to announce that we were being transferred to the home office with a big promotion. Meanwhile, I had the good fortune to get into your moon magic, so, instead of going into shock (as I'm sure my long suffering husband expected), I started gathering parchment and all the goodies for the SMOOTH MY MOVE RITUAL. I got so many hugs and pats on the head during the ritual that all my fears were dissolved. And when I started making plans and arrangements, I was delighted at how nicely things were falling into place. Al, it was an almost perfect move! We were in and settled within a week of arriving, and absolutely nothing was lost, damaged or even temporarily misplaced. My husband was so proud and pleased that he bought me the mink coat I'd been dreaming about as a thank you present. My special thanks to you and all the moon deities and spirit friends who helped!"

HOW TO MAKE YOUR OWN MOON MAGIC RITUAL TO HANDLE ANY SPECIAL SET OF CIRCUMSTANCES

When you have a problem you don't feel we've covered in the moon magic so far, the best approach is to invite the moon magic personalities to design the ritual for you. This is clearly the time for a party. First think through your problem so you can define it clearly. When you think you have it well mastered, write it out concisely. Often the process of writing it out will show you that we already have a ritual that will do the trick for you. But if you still want something different, go ahead with your party preparations. Your favorite floral oil and incense should be on your altar along with a comfortable supply of your favorite party food and drink, the written description of your problem, and the six magic squares of the moon deities. Do think of the moon personalities as your good friends, powerful and influential of course, but indeed friends for whom you really enjoy having a party.

Light your candles and incense, anoint your brow, throat, heart and solar plexus centers with the perfume oil, and begin with the MOON MAGIC AURA CLEANSING EXERCISE. There in your shaft of bright moonlight, speak: "Mother Isis, let's have a nice party and a bit of friendly discussion. Please join me now and invite all the other moon deities to be with us also." Enjoy watching your friends float down the moonbeam and become bright AURAS in your room. Next, invite your whole spirit band to join the party also. This invitation may be spoken or mental as it feels most friendly to you, but note and greet these friends as their AURAS appear with you also. When all your friends seem to be with you, lift your glass in salute and toast your friends, "Greetings good friends, I toast you in the spirit of good fellowship. Let's have a wonderful party." Then drink, and symbolically share it with all your friends by holding out your glass in the act of offering it to all.

Repeat the process with the party food, offering it to all and eating with the feeling of good fellowship. Reach out with your AURA and mentally shake hands, pat backs and hug the AURAS of your friends in the room as you continue the feeling of sharing food, drink and good fellowship in the party atmosphere. The keynote here is to enjoy! And really feel the comradeship. When you have a nice party glow, you are ready to present your problem to your friends. Speak once more to the group: "Good friends I seem to have a bit of a problem that I would like to kick around with you." Here it is best to read your written description of the situation so it will be presented clearly. When the reading is finished, continue: "I will appreciate your comments and suggestions as well as your help in planning the ritual work that may be necessary to produce the solution that will bring the highest good to all concerned. Let's continue in the party spirit as I relax and make myself alert to your answers." Then, lift your glass again and symbolically continue to share food and drink. You may get the whole picture, nothing, or anything in between during the party, but you know by now that the secret of success is just to enjoy and know that at the right time your friends will reach you with the complete message. When you feel that the session is finished, thank your friends for the joy of sharing their company, snuff your candles and go to make any necessary notes on what came through to you.

FEEDBACK FROM THE PARTY TO TAILOR A SPECIAL RITUAL

The really typical feedback on this practice is much like this one from Donald T.: "I had a very sticky problem that had not responded to the magic I tried on it. The only approach I seemed to have left was to try the party to ask my moon magic friends to help me design a special ritual to handle it. I carefully defined my problem as neatly and positively as possible and took it to the ritual party. It was a fun party. I swear I could see some of the AURAS dancing with each other, and the spirit of good fellowship was wonderful. When I got around to reading the statement of my problem, I didn't get anything that sounded like guidance. Rather, there came a big pat on my head and a very strong feeling that seemed to say, 'Don't worry about it. We'll handle it for you neatly and swiftly.' And that's just what happened. In just a couple of days, things started to happen, my stalemate was broken and things fell into place more wonderfully than anything I might have tried to engineer. Our moon magic friends are the greatest. Thanks, Al, for the introduction."

G.Y. reported what I call the alternate response: "I had a real doozie of a problem, a bit too personal in nature to relate in detail. It clearly didn't fit into the basic moon magic ritual work, so I had no choice but to try the party to get help in designing a special ritual. The response from the moon deities and my spirit people was beautiful, and right there at the party we worked out the details of a cute ritual. It took me a couple of days to gather all the goodies, but when I did, that ritual brought a feeling of complete victory which in fact took place on the material level just 5 days later. After that one, I feel I'm a pretty good moon magician."

MOON MAGIC MOTIVATORS

1. There is a moon magic solution to any problem you may encounter. If you have begun to actually practice the work of this book, its potential for good in your life should be obvious.

2. The MOTHER ISIS FIX MY FIGURE RITUAL can work wonders in the way of reshaping your figure in the direction of the ideal you set for yourself. If you don't need it now, do remember it in case you need it later.

3. Diana's ritual can lead you to a new job or new house in a very wonderful manner. Use it as often as you need it.

4. The ARTEMIS/ISHTAR RITUAL TO SMOOTH YOUR MOVE will help you whenever you need it. Use it before any physical move—you will enjoy the help to say the very least.

5. If you don't find the ritual you need in this book, moon magic can still help you solve even the trickiest of problems. Perform the party ritual to get the guidance you need to design your own ritual, and win!

15

A Lifetime Program
Of Success And Happiness
Through The Constant Application
Of Positive Moon Magic

As a successful practicing moon magician you should be leading a life of pure happiness, health, opulence, fulfillment and the regular realization of each new dream soon after you first imagine it. How shall you get from where you are right now to that exalted state of things? And how shall you be sure you can keep it all, all the rest of your life? That is the fitting windup to our study of moon lore and moon magic. In our last chapter we gave you a way to design a ritual to handle any kind of problem you may encounter. Now we must restore our balance by discussing the magical life that will never need a special ritual, that will indeed live up to the lovely biblical promise, "Before they call, I will answer, and while they are yet speaking I will hear." This is the theme of your lifetime program of successful moon magic. In this chapter I will give you all the rest of the tools; then it's up to you to use them and remain a winner evermore.

THE ESSENCE AND POWER OF LUNAR KINETICS

Success in any endeavor is clearly a matter of dynamics. Thus, we may use the terminology we are used to, and logically think of the secret of success as good lunar kinetics. When you are aware of all of life's energies and forces, and deliberately help them work to your advantage, constant success is the natural result. And isn't the name of the game piling success on top of success on top of success?

Let's look more closely at the ideas of kinetics or dynamics. Think of this as forces and energies in motion. Remember that the opposite of kinetic is static or stationary. It is the static state, the resistance to or blockage of the normal flow of energies, people and things, that causes the world's troubles. This is neatly explained by the old allegory that the reed bends (thus offering minimum resistance), but the stiff branch breaks in a strong wind. Similarly, it is the stifling of strong emotions that causes the ulcers, heart attacks and cancers that seem to be so characteristic of our modern civilization. Interestingly enough, this brings us all the way back to a restatement of the first set of natural laws I mentioned in my first book. (For those who are meeting me for the first time, this is my ninth book in this field—my first was published in 1964 and survived 9 printings.)

The two laws are complementary, or really two poles of the same principle: (1) *That which you clutch, cling to, hide, or try to withhold from others escapes from you or is diminshed in your life.* (2) *That which you willingly but intelligently display, give or share, is multiplied in your life.*

Think about it—it works with trouble, love, money, planting crops (you give the seed to the ground), a smile—it is the principle behind the practice of *tithing* that works so well for those who do it in the right spirit. It is also the principle of lunar kinetics that will maintain your dynamic balance of the flowing energies, and so promote your continued growth and well being. Take the time to meditate on these simple truths until you have really made them a part of you. This is the foundation of your new magical life of happiness, success and the fulfillment of all your dreams.

PREVENTIVE MEDICINE—THE LUNAR KINETICS SUPER RITUAL

Let's go back to the last chapter where we planned a party to get the guidance to tailor your ritual to handle any special problem. It's a beautiful ritual and it works, but I honestly had a twinge of guilt about putting it in there, and I wouldn't have had I not known that we would get to this section right away. Stop to think about it. All the way through this book we've been asking our moon deity and spirit friends for help, but what have we done for them in return? True, their needs are not nearly the same as ours, and there is not much we can do for them, but the spirit of carrying your own weight and wanting to reciprocate for their help is of the utmost importance. Thus, the LUNAR KINETICS SUPER RITUAL is a party, just like the one where you ask for help in designing a special ritual, with this one super difference— you don't ask for anything! Instead, you thank your friends for their wonderful and continuous help, enjoy the spirit of genuine friendship, and ask if there is anything you can do for them.

Obviously, this should be one of the very first rituals that you devote yourself to, and it should be repeated as a friendly celebration on the night of each new and full moon. The normal response to your question or offer of help will be something like a pat on the head and/or a friendly hug along with the feeling of "We're fine, just keep striving for growth as you do your best to live a life of light and inspiration to your fellow beings." But, if you are straying from the positive path, you may well get a gentle suggestion that you clean up your act. And, very occasionally, your friends may have a pet project or two that they would like you to work for or contribute to. Since it is the work of the moon deities through E.S.P Laboratory that caused this book to be created, your friends may suggest that you request its free literature and consider affiliating, and hopefully there will be local groups of mutual benefit as well, but we will cover that in our concluding section. The thought we want to stress here is simply that super power and super effectiveness in all of your life expression as well as your moon magic work comes from the adult approach of mutuality and reciprocation, never from the "gimme, gimme, gimme" approach of the selfish child. But, as you enjoy the LUNAR KINETICS SUPER RITUAL PARTY, and make it a real joy for your spirit and moon deity friends, you will find a whole new dimension of happiness, progress and fulfill-ment permeating every nook and cranny of your life.

RESULTS FROM THE LUNAR KINETICS SUPER RITUAL

J.R. sent us this report on the SUPER RITUAL: "My parties for the moon magic friends were fun from the very first one, and you're quite right that most of the time you get a pat on the head and a hug for your offer to help them. But then there came a time when I sort of got called to task. The strong feeling that came when I offered help was like: 'You are far too serious about that special project on your job. Go get your blood pressure taken if you have any doubts, but do immediately put things in perspec-tive and relax. Otherwise, you will shortly have a stroke or a heart attack.' There just happened to be one of those mobile blood pressure places nearby, so I trotted over right after the ritual and got quite a shock. My blood pressure was 260 over 140! And they wanted to hospitalize me! Somehow I escaped and went right back to my altar. I invited my friends back to thank them for the warning and let them help me get the stifled energies flowing properly. It took just a few minutes to realize the errors in my assumptions and clear my spleen and solar plexus chakra blocks. Then, at spirit suggestion, I had a nice big belt of brandy for a nightcap and settled down for some more instruction on the astral while my body was asleep. A week later I had my blood pressure rechecked—believe it or not it was a healthy 129 over 88! I think I owe my very physical existence to my moon deity and spirit friends and that party ritual."

E.D. sent us this one: "Al, you already know that my life membership in E.S.P. Lab was suggested to me at a SUPER LUNAR KINETICS RITUAL PARTY and I still feel that that's the nicest thing that ever happened to me, but I have a fresh experience from the same ritual that I just have to share with you. The ritual part has almost always been only a super good time, but this time I felt that my offer of help was accepted. The strong feeling was: 'Your acquaintance, P., is in a very deep depression and there is some danger of a suicide. Please call P. and arrange dinner together for tomorrow night. Your positive influence will be enough to pull him out of it.' As soon as the party was over, I followed instructions and called P. My dinner invitation was accepted. It took all my power of positive AURA control to keep P. from dragging me down to that depressed level when we met, but I knew I had a lot of spirit help so I hung in there. And when we parted, P. was snapped out of the depression and back on the path of usefulness and growth. Al, that would have been reward enough itself, especially with the enthusiastic pats and hugs I got from my spirit friends on the way home. But they also seem to have a way of saying a very tangible extra thank you. This time it was an out of the blue windfall of $2,200 that was unmistakably their thank you gift. This lunar kinetics life is the greatest!"

EXPANDING YOUR LOVE AFFAIR WITH
THE MOON DEITIES TO A LOVE AFFAIR
WITH ALL OF LIFE

In case you haven't thought of it that way, you are, or very soon will be, involved in a delicious love affair with your spirit band and the moon magic personalities. With some of the special personalities it can be very sensual, or should we say super sensual. But with all of them, you will feel a love that is honestly stronger than the normal love between brothers and sisters. If you don't feel the relationship already, a few of the happy parties we discussed in our last section will make it more and more real to you. And this is indeed a big step toward fitting more comfortably and effectively into your magical new life. As you love and feel loved by these wonderful spirit beings and moon personalities, their tender concern for all of earth's creatures will start to rub off on you until you realize that you have joined them in a thrilling love affair will all of life.

You will be amazed at the "magical" difference! Life and all of its creatures will reciprocate your love, and treat you with the same respect and tenderness that you are showing them. Yes, there will be a fresh level of harmlessness to your path through life—it's not necessary to go to extremes of vegetarianism or refusing to bathe because it might kill the tiny creatures infesting your skin as we hear that some of the eastern sects do, but you will consciously avoid unnecessary killing or harm to any creature. There is a danger here of slipping into something of a starry-eyed mystic state that wants you to abdicate your worldly responsibilities in order to go and seek your guru, or perhaps just sit in blissful mystic meditation. But it is to be recognized as just that, a danger! You are here to grow into a highly successful moon magician, and it can only be done by striving within the framework of your immediate situation. The only way to buy your time or anything else without destroying the very thing you seek is by your growth and expertise as a moon magician. To run, no matter how noble and mystic may seem the temptation, is to lose it all, but to stand and strive with the loving help of your moon deity and spirit friends is the path of certain victory.

Let nothing deter you from your balanced growth and improving ability as a moon magician. Harmlessness in no way means that you should be a patsy, or that it is improper to remove stubborn obstacles with whatever force is necessary, but you must never do it in anger or with vindictiveness. There is no way to sweep the truth under the rug, your spirit and moon deity friends will always know the truth, and their cooperation and help depends on you doing your best. But that is all you need do— your best within the framework of your understanding and emotional condition of the time. You need never cry over or be ashamed of a mistake, only learn from it, that you may not pull the same goof again. And you will find yourself quickly slipping into the happy and effective life of a true moon magician.

FEEDBACK ON THE MAGIC OF ONENESS WITH ALL LIFE

This is another of those spots where it is hard to select a standout bit of feedback. We get so many reports that are similar—similarly wonderful that is—that the selection process is like reaching into a grab bag knowing that whatever you get is good, but wondering if you may be missing something better. Let's let this one from G.K. represent the hundreds of good letters that were in my grab bag: "Al, this love affair with life thing is magnificent magic! Since I started to really feel it, the whole world has seemed to bend over backwards to be super nice to me. In this busy city, complete strangers have suddenly started to smile and open doors for me where I have always been ignored before. Sales clerks and even government officials have become super helpful and attentive. All manner of small animals seem to seek me out to share affection. The magic extends to fun things like winning door prizes wherever I go. I wake up thinking of a number about once a month, then play it and win! I used to drag myself out of bed in the morning, not at all ready to cope with my dull life, but now I bound out of bed eagerly looking forward to the joys of the day. And you are so right. Since all this started I haven't thought of doing a ritual to ask for something—somehow my needs are anticipated and I have what I want or need before I realize what I'm supposed to do with it! Al, I agree with you that when we are finished with these bodies we must be destined to go on to a nicer place, but I'm sure not in any hurry! Life is wonderful for me right here and right now! Please tell everybody for me how nice the moon magic love affair with life can be!"

HOW TO LIVE THE CHARMED AND MAGICAL LIFE FOREVERMORE

All too often, the student reaches ths happy point and gets so distracted by the riches and material pleasures that he soon forgets what caused it, and over a period of time the little bad habits begin to reappear until one day the magic is all gone and he wakes up in some kind of misery. If it hurts enough, it will push him to look for help and so turn him back to magic. The parable of the prodigal son applies here; his spirit and moon deity friends will not turn their backs on him, but will greet him with open arms and he will be on his way back up again. Not a real sad story, but quite typical of the average student's progress, a sort of sine curve just full of ups and downs. Let's not let this be you! Your proper destiny is the happy magical life forever. Isn't it worth a little extra effort to keep it so?

Our direction comes from the basic law, *That which you willingly but intelligently display, give or share is multiplied in your life*. Thus you need to share your magic, but with intelligence so you don't make yourself look like a kook and turn people off. Of course your most effective teaching method is the happy example of your own successes. Let your success and obvious happiness shine forth so that your friends and acquaintances will want to ask you what is your secret. Then explain it simply and carefully, in terms that your questioner is ready to understand. And every life you uplift in the process will surely uplift you as well.

Another important part of sharing is group work. We need to associate with and work magically with others of like mind. A local group is nice, and if you can't find one, you may do well by organizing a group of your own. I will be happy to help you with this if you ask me. But you should also be involved on the national or international level. And here I would be remiss if I did not suggest that you consider affiliating with E.S.P. Laboratory, the group I head under the guidance and direction of the moon personalities who are now our mutual friends. I would be delighted to see that you get our free introductory literature, and to enjoy reading your personal feedback on results of your own successful moon magic, or to help you trouble-shoot your magical work. Feel free to write me, Al G. Manning, c/o E.S.P. Laboratory, 7559 Santa Monica Blvd., Los Angeles, California 90046. I promise that I will joyfully respond.

```
1987 UPDATE - AL MANNING'S
CURRENT MAILING ADDRESS
% E.S.P. LAB OF TEXAS
P.O.BOX 216
EDGEWOOD, TX 75117
```

MOON MAGIC MOTIVATORS

1. You should be leading a magical life of pure success, happiness, riches, health and love, In this chapter we give you all the rest of the tools to make it so for you now.

2. Lunar super kinetics is the essence and power of your magic. Meditate on its two complementary laws until you have made them a part of you.

3. Carrying your own weight as an adult is all it takes to launch your charmed life. Use the LUNAR KINETICS SUPER RITUAL PARTY as a big part of your share of the load. Perform the party ritual at least every new and full moon.

4. The LUNAR KINETICS SUPER RITUAL PARTIES will quickly build your love affair with your moon deity and spirit friends. Let this grow and expand into a love affair with all of life.

5. Your love affair with life will set you up as somebody special and the whole world will cooperate in making your personal life one of magic, good luck and charm.

6. Don't forget what is causing your good fortune. Share your magic in personal and group work, and insure that you will live a charmed life forevermore.

7. I invite your feedback and questions. Feel free to write me personally at the address given above. I promise to respond promptly.